Topical Building

Topical Building

The Work of Hugh Cullum Architects

Contents

Introduction

Thoughts on Practice

Hugh Cullum

One of the reasons for writing this book is to have the opportunity to look back over the past forty or so years of practice and draw some conclusions about where we should be heading next—a bit like a sailor who looks at his boat's wake to see where he has actually travelled relative to his intended heading.

I think "open" is an appropriate way to describe our approach to our work. It connotes a degree of "not yet decided" as well as an eagerness to take on board whatever a commission may bring, whether from the client, or from the physical or cultural context. With this goes an unwillingness to restrict and pin down the wider brief of a project. Although we sometimes undertake a degree of explicit analysis of client requirements, context and so forth, we find that the reality is actually so complex and layered that it usually eludes this kind of methodical procedure, or is distorted and flattened by it.

The general public understandably expects the architect to bring a degree of rigour and logical thought to a project, but all too often this is seen as a narrow methodology. When architects present their ideas, they sometimes do so very defensively, presenting design as having been the inevitable outcome of a logical process, as though we were the dullest kind of engineers, dependent on the classic diagram of site constraints and the bubble drawing of client requirements.

This way of operating is sometimes taken up a notch and the architect invents a kind of metalogic which presents design as a process of revelation. This gives rise to another sort of diagram, often full of geometrical transformations—foldings, reflections, subtraction and addition of primary solids and, if you have Neoplatonist inclinations, significant numbers and proportions.

I can see the attraction of this last modus operandi. It gives the architect a certain confidence and has great pedigree—its has been a mainstay of the architectural tradition and gives a kind of framework, or the rules of a game, through which creativity and invention can be exercised.

Too often, though, these kinds of exercises are constructed after the event or unwittingly superimposed on it, bringing a false neatness and the illusion of control.

By contrast, I am quite happy to describe the way I work as being more like feeling my way in the dark. The path is there and the objects to negotiate are real, but they do not reveal themselves except by my reaching out tentatively until something tangible is discovered. Bit by bit, the picture is built up, brought more sharply into focus and reviewed until the whole building is described.

Colin St John "Sandy" Wilson describes his own experience of design as, "the interaction of two agents in a reiterative process of discovery... an exchange of energies between a creative discipline and the tentative realisation of a way of life...".[1]

A "reiterative exchange of energies"? This is a long way from a method or process and perfectly captures the impossibility of pinning down how an architect (or a painter or a poet) works. The relationship between "living" and "a building" is complex and difficult. They are different categories and can only be related, in anything other than a superficial or mechanistic way, through building's being a kind of poetic metaphor.

This relationship between living and a building is discussed, albeit in the context of a Baroque palace, in the concluding section of my doctoral dissertation on the Northern Italian Palace of Venaria Reale. The discussion works within an analytical framework derived from Heidegger, Ricoeur and Gadamer and developed by the architectural teachers Peter Carl and Dalibor Vesely. If pressed for a philosophy underlying my approach to architecture, this is where I would point.

I shall attempt to give a brief synopsis of the argument.

The proper role of a work of art, and that includes the role of any architecture with representational aspirations (which certainly describes the Palace of Venaria) is, following Aristotle, the mimesis of being. It is to be a mirror showing the nature of life. The action in a play, for example, is potent because it is recognised as being, in some sense, paradigmatic; as illustrating a universal truth about being. In this sense we are invited to 'step outside' being to see more clearly its true nature. This is the heightened reality that a play brings to us and this is, following Gadamer, the essence of symbolic representation.

This, though, brings us to an inherent paradox. Because we, the observers of the play, are confined within immanent reality we are, by definition, unable properly to 'step outside' this, to be able to look back at it in a holistic sense. Such a view, which one senses with the paradigmatic, can only be hinted at, somehow implied or evoked through poetry, symbol or metaphor. It can never be wholly described or pinned down. Vesely's concept of "divided representation" refers to the attempt to do exactly this by mistakenly believing that a seductively powerful system of instrumental representation, such as mathematics or perspective, can fully control and describe reality. There is a tendency for the internal consistency and related rules of representation to become more trusted, and thus more important, than the ground of experience itself, which can be seen as ambiguous and thereby untrustworthy. In the case of Venaria, the system of representation under investigation was that of Baroque rhetoric, which is seen as completely controlling and pervading every aspect of the palace—its architecture, painting, sculpture, garden, and plays and rituals. Venaria comes very close to being

an entirely instrumental representation and is only rescued by its overarching religious and dynastic aims.

Venaria is perhaps a forerunner of what Vesely sees as the fundamental modern problem of divided representation. In contemporary architecture, this is reflected in a misguided concern for control and predictability of result. By contrast, Vesely and Carl suggest that architecture should be concerned with the much less certain enterprise of creating the paradigmatic setting, which they describe as "situation". In Vesely's words, "situation is not an event, image, representation, symbol or structure, but all of these brought together in such a way that they constitute a territory... rooted in a concrete level of existence...". Through providing a setting which, to paraphrase Ricoeur, points towards or reveals the paradigmatic situation, architecture is symbolic.

My approach to architecture owes a great debt to the teaching of Peter Carl and Dalibor Vesely, both of whom came to Cambridge when I was a student there under Sandy Wilson's professorship. Peter and Dalibor were my studio masters in my final years and, with Peter, I went on to write my PhD on symbolic representation in the Northern Italian Baroque.

When I graduated I went to work for Sandy in London where I was lucky enough to be cast as a sort of 'page-boy', running round after Sandy, interpreting his sketches and making endless, enormous card models. It was my experience at his office that taught me the necessity for constant refinement, iteration and review through all and whatever means of representation were available. And even when all this is done, the building itself is alarmingly and excitingly quite different from what one expected.

Altogether, my formative years left me with a far from simplistic appreciation of what architecture could be, and a love of complex domes and staircases which I hope is not too evident in the work of the practice.

After a couple of years with Sandy, I started a small practice with Richard Nightingale. Our bread and butter was domestic renovation and extension (as it continues to be), but we were lucky enough to win a competition for the new British High Commission in Nairobi, a major commission which really put us on the map and gave us the credibility to land commissions for new buildings, such as the library and teaching block for the Central School of Speech and Drama, the new headquarters building for Warr's Harley-Davidson and the flagship shop for Graff Diamonds in New Bond Street.

Both at Cullum and Nightingale and now, with my own solo practice, most commissions have been gained through direct recommendations or word of mouth. Hugh Cullum Architects do almost no advertising and have a low public profile. I'm not sure in any case that our built work is immediately photogenic or sufficiently stylistically coherent for us to promote a house

Above: Sandy Wilson in the entrance hall of the British Library

style (although I'm sure there are recognisable quirks and preoccupations common to all our projects).

Our most successful work has been in collaboration with visionary clients, all of whom had strong ideas which have resulted in quite diverse projects. A couple of them are particularly memorable.

Professor Michael Marland was the headteacher at North Westminster School, an inner-city school of 2,000 students, many from disadvantaged backgrounds. His energy and charisma were such that he managed to persuade the likes of Jessye Norman and Willard White to perform at the school, and Margaret Drabble and Fay Weldon to come and talk to his students. With an eye to extracting the maximum from slender resources he commissioned us to design a low-budget temporary music space on a disused oil-tank enclosure. An architect *manqué* (a claim he often made) he took huge pleasure in collaborating in the design of what was really a refined shed with aspirations to being a concert hall.

Similarly driven, though quite different, was Laurence Graff, the diamond merchant whose passion for diamonds saw him rise from a back-room assistant in Hatton Garden to an immensely wealthy international jeweller. In the 1990s we built his first shop in New Bond Street. This is *the* place to be for luxury fine jewellery and the flagship shop signalled his arrival to the big-time. We have recently demolished, expanded and rebuilt his first shop and built several more in the Far East.

For both these clients, and for many others, we have built a number of projects over several years and the process has been one of balanced collaboration. Knowing a client over a long period of time allows a degree of trust to be built up and for the establishment of a dialogue that gives a deep understanding of the needs and aspirations, voiced or otherwise, of the client.

We have become increasingly involved in architectural conservation over the past few years. No doubt this is partly because conservation movements have now become so much more visible, but it is also an aspect of our own increasing attention to the cultural context and setting of our projects, a good many of which are in central London and involve historic buildings. Without being too puritanical, we have always aimed for our buildings to be 'well made', believing that architectural tectonics and craftsmanship reveal the care and effort in the making of a building. These qualities are often much more apparent in old buildings where the relative simplicity of construction makes them more easily read and appreciated and, of course, they are largely handmade, rather than being the assembly of machine-made components.

The evidence of care and thought in a building reveals the humanity of those who built it and I would be pleased to find, 50 years on, that the consideration and effort we and our clients had put into a project were still evident and valued.

Top: Music room for North Westminster Community School (with Cullum and Nightingale) **Bottom:** Staircase at Jewellery Salon, 1996

1   Wilson, Colin St John, *Architectural Reflections: Studies in the Philosophy and Practice of Architecture*, Manchester: Manchester University Press, 2000, p 32.

Ceiling survey, Inigo Jones' Queen's House, Greenwich

Style and Non-Style

Alan Powers

"The style is the man himself", said the Count de Buffon in the eighteenth century, contradicting the received views that style was ordained by God and Nature, and epitomised in the classical tradition. Hugh Cullum admits that he doesn't have a 'house style' in his practice. The admission recognises the common view that consistency of a certain obvious kind is something to be aimed for. Anyone who studies the history of architecture tends to make that assumption, since it represents the large ideas that structure understanding of this activity.

Classical and Gothic were the twin variants of a load-bearing masonry architecture that dominated Western culture for the best part of more than 2,000 years. When at the beginning of the twentieth century they were deemed no longer viable models to follow, it was not easy to know where to go next. After the first thrill of breaking the old rules of symmetry and stripping away the decoration, it became clear, as Mies van der Rohe declared, that although everything was changed, it was "neither necessary nor useful to invent a new architecture every Monday morning". At its best, the realisation of a new form of classicism in the language of steel and glass made for buildings as compelling as any that had gone before, but as visual and constructional clichés, they could also be inappropriate and tedious.

The history of modernism has been told in many ways, but only relatively recently with all its richness of nuance. There were polemical reasons for emphasising the radical nature of the break with the past, yet the feelings engendered by past buildings and some of the architectural methods used to achieve them were, as we now realise, buried within most of the exemplars of the new way of building, Mies included. The uneasy relationship between modern architecture and the past began to surface more frequently in the years after 1945, which, despite the passage of time, still marks in many ways the beginning of the present period in architecture. This is particularly the case with Hugh Cullum who, like most architects working today, is only at one or two removes of influence from the post-war generation.

Colin St John Wilson was Professor at Cambridge during Hugh's years there and it was with Wilson that Hugh got his first job, working up models and sketch designs for the New British Library. Wilson belonged to a generation that thought it had inherited a modern architecture already formed, but came over time to realise that there was scope for much more variation. The emptiness of much modern architecture left the majority of non-architects baffled and the anger of critics such as Ian Nairn broke the walls of their professional citadel.

Hugh was of an age to participate in a major process of transformation that took place at Cambridge and marked several generations, in which the theoretical, political and methodological edifice of modernism seemed to grow hollow and fade away. Wilson, to his great credit, embraced and, to a considerable extent, promoted this change and its influence is reflected in the shift of emphasis undergone during Wilson's development of the British Library between its first inception on the St Pancras site in 1979 and the final version completed in 1998. However, what his successors have accomplished goes well beyond the shaking up of the pieces implied in Wilson's definition of "The Other Tradition in Modern Architecture".

While the term postmodernism implies a reaction, what we can trace in Hugh's account of his studies with Dalibor Vesley and Peter Carl was more like a transformation from within rather than an about-turn. Following the discipline of phenomenology, it was an intense process of reading, thinking and designing, examining the nature of perception and response, and, from this, reconstructing a more grounded and meaningful architectural practice.

I think it is difficult for those who appreciate the results of this process of rethinking, but did not share in it, to see quite how it worked. As Hugh has written, "Vesely and Carl suggest that architecture should be concerned with the much less certain enterprise of creating the paradigmatic setting, which they describe as 'situation'." In Vesely's words, "situation is not an event, image, representation, symbol or structure, but all of these brought together in such a way that they constitute a territory... rooted in a concrete level of existence...". If the ideas involved were at times complex ones, the results were of a kind likely to appeal to a public among whom the more rigid forms of modernism had reached a nadir. The work of Eric Parry, perhaps the chief flag-bearer of the Vesley-Carl studio, bears this out. From the beginning, his buildings echoed the ethics of the Arts and Crafts movement, with the same address to materials as active participants in the quality emanating from the finished product.

Since the Gothic Revival with its novel insistence on a single correct style in the mid nineteenth century, the activity of designing in what appear to be different styles has been seen as an absence of principle. After a later period of eclecticism, the modern movement brought back a similar restrictiveness in its critical outlook. Or did it? The definition of modern architecture simply by style has become a form of tautology—what looks modern is modern, no further questions asked. It has taken a long time to realise how much reference and meaning was included in these appearances, and how far from superficial were the ways in which architects such as Berthold Lubetkin or Ernö Goldfinger were working in England from the 1930s to the 1960s. Each of these architects, whose posthumous celebrity may well reflect their attunement to our latter-day conditions, were part of a flowing process of discovery, neither rigid nor dogmatic. It is this open rather than closed approach that Hugh defines in relation to his experience working for Sandy Wilson, "It was my experience at his office that taught me the necessity for constant refinement, iteration and review through all and whatever means of representation were available. And even when all this is done the building itself is alarmingly and excitingly quite different from what one expected."

Opinion in the British Isles is antagonistic towards the brand of modern architecture that many designers would like to practice and shows little sign of changing. Critics might argue that architects bow too readily to the demands of planning and conservation authorities that they play nice and to keep out of trouble—concessions that go against the combative stance associated with modernism. The results that are often encouraged by planners as responses to the demand to work alongside existing buildings can indeed be deplorable. However, there is a growing canon of projects in which a more culturally intelligent and imaginative understanding of context have led to the production of clever,

serviceable and aesthetically delightful elevations, spaces and interiors. These brighten our lives and our streets without hitting wrong notes.

To do this requires a certain humility in the architect, but achieving this is perhaps part of the lesson of phenomenology, that discipline of self-abnegation and careful listening. This should not deny the architect's ability to synthesise many aspects of a project into a coherent whole and to anticipate as yet unarticulated needs.

Reviewing an earlier project by Cullum and Nightingale in 1996, a Hampstead house for the artist Sean Stanley, the critic Naomi Stungo related her enjoyment of the playful interior to a wider issue of the role of architecture in society, writing that "it still seems, in a country where vast numbers of people feel completely alienated by and disengaged from their surroundings, that thinking about ways in which architecture can be used to make people involved in their environment is, and will continue to be, an extremely important issue".

Even today, some 20 years later, an architect such as Cullum, who is equally at ease with the modern interior of his St Michael's Community Hall as he is with the neo-classical design of his New Bond Street jewellery shopfront, risks being deemed insincere or worse for failing to adhere to a narrow, orthodox and stylistically consistent definition of modernity. This is a naive view of the architect as hero that has been responsible for much damage to people and to places. Incomprehension has been the fate of some British architects of the interwar period and after, such as HS Goodhart-Rendel and Oliver Hill, who, in different ways and with different motives, switched between modernism and historic styles and performed well in both areas. For Goodhart-Rendel, modernism's promise of freedom had turned its followers into "inconscient slaves of their own styleless stylism". Every building, he argued, should be judged on its own merits. The questions to ask were "was the style chosen well?" and "has it been used intelligently?"

At the time that Cullum was studying at Cambridge, I was writing my undergraduate thesis on Goodhart-Rendel for the History of Art course in the same building, divided by a fairly impenetrable if invisible partition between the disciplines. Perhaps, 40 years on in the wider world, that wall has finally begun to come down and there is a new turn of the wheel. Indeed, in 2016, Goodhart-Rendel was included in an exhibition at the Royal Academy under the title "Mavericks". He was in good company with Hawksmoor and Charles Holden, whose work he admired, and James Stirling, who came too late for him to form an opinion.

Unless they suddenly land a whale, Hugh Cullum and his studio are not competing on the scale of these authors of massive projects, but it is somehow concordant with the philosophy that they follow that doing small things well is enough. It is their approach and attitude that is distinctive, regardless of whether the work is at the scale of a symphony or of a more modest, but no less demanding, chamber work.

Craft and Material

Well Mount Studios

Above and previous page: Painting room, Well Mount Studios

Well Mount Studios

Hugh Cullum

We had built the painter Shaun Stanley's house in 1993–1994 from the ruins of an ancient laundry in Hampstead. Initially he painted in an annex but, a few years later, he was able to buy a property nearby at 2 Well Mount Studios, which, although badly converted into a house, was once the studio of Mark Gertler (1891–1939). I had set up my own solo practice by then and Shaun asked me to make the building into his studio.

Certain aspects of the design were givens. Although Shaun bought the building as a house it had previously been a studio and it was inevitable that the original layout would be followed to make a large top-lit volume as the main painting space.

Shaun also wanted an apartment on the site to offer to guests. Rather than steal any of the ground floor, we dug beneath the studio to make a one-bedroom apartment. The main problem with underground spaces is getting enough light to them. In this building, the treatment of light is key to articulating the relation of the major spaces and the way they are occupied. It enables the hierarchy of the spaces to be clearly read in terms of their relative importance and also in terms of what might, in former times and in those edifices, have been identified as their degree of sacredness.

This hierarchy places the activity of painting and printmaking above that of everyday living. The main painting room has a generous band of north-facing patent glazing, which provides most of the light, and three windows onto the street. The windows and north-emanating light can be screened with translucent blinds creating a soft white light that falls evenly on every surface, making the studio calm and completely isolated. Off the studio and a couple of steps down is the print room, again top-lit but with sinks and benches and a view onto the entry courtyard. It is a cross between a kitchen and a laboratory, and definitely a space for doing rather than contemplation.

The lower-ground floor living spaces literally share the same light as the studio. Light passes through the main space of the painting room before being channelled down into the space below through a kind of light cell. This construction allows the lower space a 'presence' in the studio and provides the main blank white backdrop against which the activity of painting takes place. To the side of the painting screen is a discreet window vitrine, and if you look up from the lower space it gives some clue as to what is happening in the space above (dependent on how communicative Shaun decides to be in choosing its content).

Broadly speaking, the materiality of the apartment and the studio reinforce the hierarchy described by the treatment of light and this is particu-

Cumberland slate stairs and courtyard, Well Mount Studios

larly evident in the entrance hall where the visitor goes up into the studio or down to the apartment. The stairs to the studio are playful and light. Their structure suggests a suspension of disbelief (a humble miracle) while the balustrade is an ascending series of square steel frames with glass infill hinting at the as yet empty canvases waiting in the studio beyond. The stairs to the basement apartment are simple, unelaborated Cumbrian slate slabs.

Seen from within the studio, the entrance from the staircase is a flat white door, set completely flush and without detail, in the perimeter wall. The whole side wall of the studio is made into cupboards which form a flush white surface for hanging drawings and prints. The numerous openings in the perimeter are all concealed and when you shut the door to the studio behind you there is a sense of complete isolation. Even the staircase down to the wine cellar is concealed as a trapdoor in the maple flooring.

Like a piano lid opened at the start of a recital, the lid of the wine cellar stairs is opened and balanced on a thin stick. A hidden button is pressed and a motorised staircase is lowered into the wine cellar for the ritual retrieval of a couple of bottles. The wine cellar is furnished with a simple glazed basin and a couple of chairs. It could be considered the perfect complement to the space above; the studio is smooth, white and ethereal, while the cellar is dark, primitive and mysterious, its unfinished surfaces witness to the long and arduous process of reimagining the building and carving out the new space below.

Shaun was a constant collaborator and critic during the design stage and made sure he was absolutely convinced of the rightness of our proposals before allowing us to draw up the building for construction. He remained stubbornly unpersuaded by any attempt to talk him into anything without first having it thoroughly described with sketch drawings and a great many huge card models, which we made primarily to show how the light worked. Later on, Shaun was also very involved in the building work and visited the site daily, sometimes even mucking in with the workforce on jobs like floor-sanding. It obviously preoccupied him and a number of his paintings have the building work as subject matter. One shows a dark infernal scene with strange figures and machinery busy at work with picks and shovels. Three plotting figures, whom one might imagine to be the architect, client and builder, appear in the corner of the canvas.

I have particular sympathy for this painting because I cannot claim to have an easy love of building sites in Britain. I was brought up in North America and my early impressions of building sites were that they were rather magical places smelling of fresh-cut spruce and cedar shingles, where building was dry, fast and relatively accurate.

By contrast, the British sites I became involved with in my small-scale practice were usually refurbishment jobs where the sites were dirty, cold

Top: Hatch to wine cellar stair, Well Mount Studios **Bottom:** Retractable wine cellar stair, Well Mount Studios

and chaotic. Shaun's site at Well Mount was certainly one of these, with a massive amount of underpinning of the existing main walls of the building and with interlocking piling around the sunken courtyard light well. It seemed to take months and the removal of innumerable skip-loads of sticky clay before anything vaguely recognisable as our design began to emerge. This, and other jobs like it, instilled in me huge respect for any architect who can wrest order out of the chaos that is British building. To have the willpower and strength of character to balance the world of the building site with that of the client, and to extract a worthwhile piece of building, is admirable.

This mucky process of building, though, is an essential constituent of the identity of the product and its architectural value. Mud, swearing and sweat are the prices paid to wrestle with the remnants of an existing building and make them conform to the purpose of a new one. It is good to be reminded of this and at Shaun's studio we were unabashed in the exposure of the underpinning and concrete in primary spaces like the wine cellar and on the walls of the sunken courtyard. I should add, too, that the whole process of building was, in this case, considerably eased by the skill and helpful attitude of the builder, David Lightfoot.

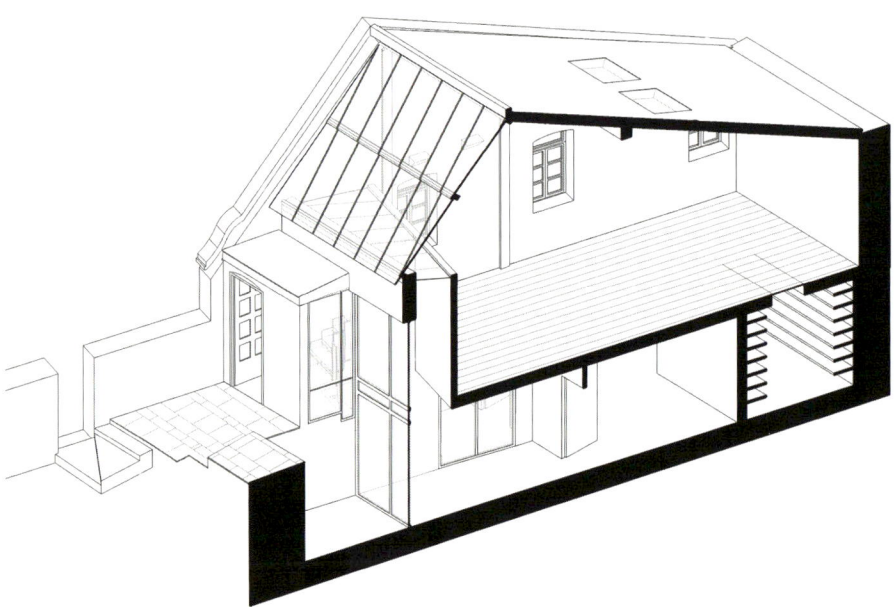

Top: Shaun Stanley, *Construction Scene*, gouache **Bottom:** Sectional axonometric, Well Mount Studios
Opposite: Staircase from basement flat, Well Mount Studios

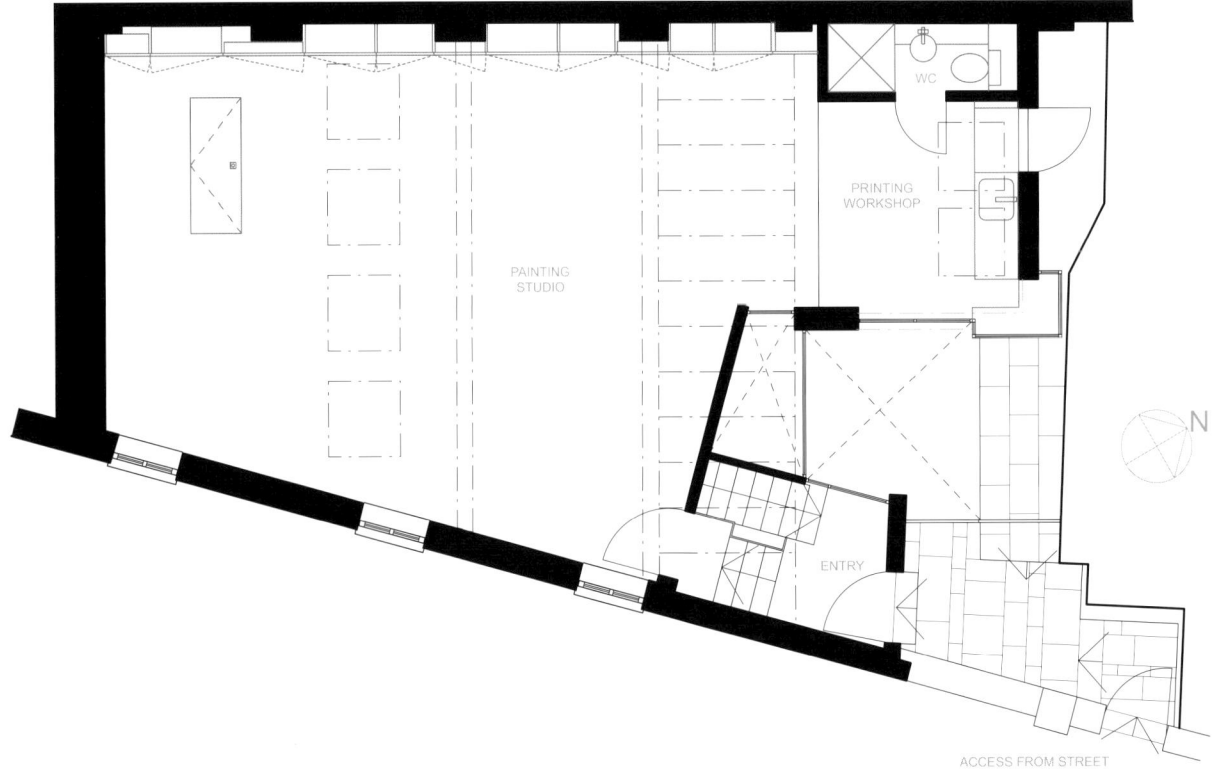

PAINTING
STUDIO

PRINTING
WORKSHOP

WC

ENTRY

N

ACCESS FROM STREET

Ground floor plan, Well Mount Studios

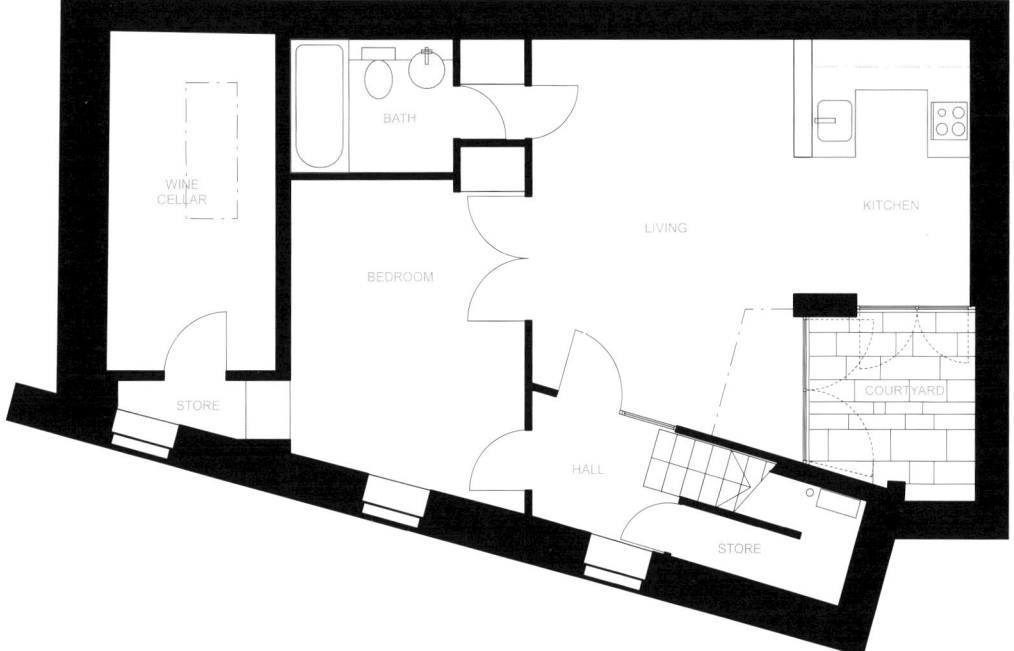

WINE
CELLAR

BATH

STORE

BEDROOM

LIVING

KITCHEN

COURTYARD

HALL

STORE

 N

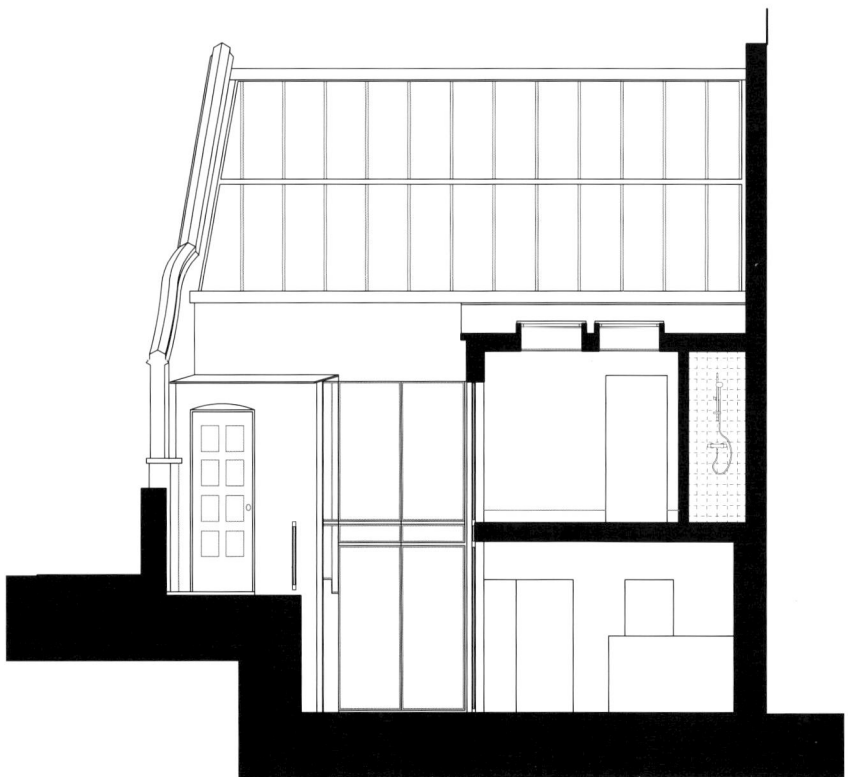

Section through courtyard, Well Mount Studios

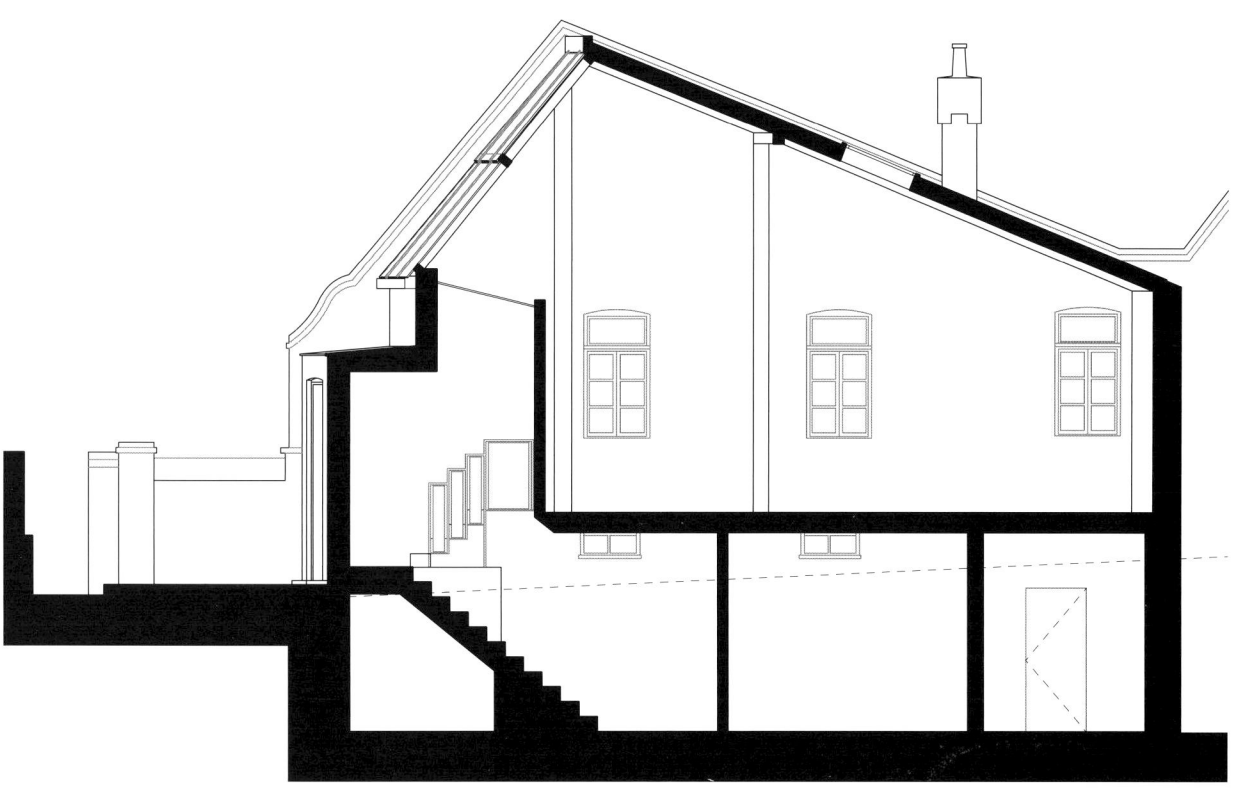

Long section through painting room, Well Mount Studios

Material, Craft and Decorative Difficulties

Charles Rattray

The subtitle for this section of *Topical Building* is sufficient to make architects start. Not the mention of material; there we may for the moment agree with Breuer that "the basis of modern architecture... is not the new materials, nor even the new form, but the new mentality".[1] No: it is the mention of craft. For craft is supposed to be dead, buried alongside its friend, ornament, a hundred years ago. Reports of its death appear to have been greatly exaggerated.

Of course there is no physical experience of architecture without building, and there is no building without materials assembled with some degree of craft. This truism has exceptional—one might almost say alchemic—consequences. Behind it lie the roots of architectural creativity: all the myriad judgements made in the light of precedent, technology, context, programme (and so on), the creative awareness of constraints as well as possibilities, and those transformative critical reflections that are common to all serious artists. In our present context, in other words, it is Hugh Cullum's remarkable architectural intelligence that renders his materials emotionally communicative. But let us wait to discuss that. First, let us ponder this interest in craft or, perhaps more accurately, craft 'in general' because it is a subject that gives rise to a considerable degree of architectural angst, and for reasons that are as much artistic as commercial.

For example, in the twentieth century, the richest and most technologically developed countries—those of the so-called First World—can be seen to echo the dominant culture of the century—modernism—in its enthusiasm for (some would say worship of) standardisation and the machine. They employ a synthetic building industry foreseen in the nineteenth century that brings together off-the-shelf products manufactured in bulk. Far from regarding this as a problem, from the 1950s on Alison and Peter Smithson solemnly embraced such 'as-found' products, materials and conditions, describing this as a "New Brutalism". Then, after

a few decades in the doldrums, their attitude became an exemplar for a new generation of influential English practices, among them some characterised a decade ago as "Gritty Brits".[2] For such architects, craft is equivalent to anachronistic self-indulgence.

Where craft does continue to be discussed is in the world of architectural conservation and repair, an area necessarily preoccupied with the building methods and decorative practices of the past. One might argue that this is partly why conservation is sometimes seen as old hat and not 'real' architecture. Either way, there are further connections, since talk of repair immediately reminds us of those founding members of the Society for the Protection of Ancient Buildings (SPAB) in 1877, John Ruskin and William Morris—men who are more famous as heroic, if ultimately unsuccessful, warriors in the Arts and Crafts movement's battle to stem the tide of industrialisation. Theirs was the story of Mrs Partington's mop all over again. So it was that in 1895, the year before he died, a despondent Morris could write: "Now that I am grown old and see that nothing can be done, I half wish that I had not been born with a sense of romance and beauty in this accursed age".[3]

But the break with craft was not absolute. The tensions between handicraft and industrial processes are illustrated—surprisingly in the light of his pre-First World War practice—by Walter Gropius. On becoming Director of the Bauhaus in 1919, he stated in words worthy of W. R. Lethaby:

> Artists, sculptors, painters, we must all return to handwork!... There is no difference in kind between the artist and the craftsman. The artist is an enhancement of the craftsman. The grace of heaven, in rare moments of inspiration, which lie beyond the control of his will, causes art to blossom unconsciously from the work of his hand. But a foundation in handwork is indispensable for every artist.... Let us therefore establish a new guild of craftsmen.[4]

Perhaps it was a short-lived enthusiasm: by 1963, Gropius' recollection was much closer to statements of the *Deutscher Werkbund* from 50 years earlier, namely that, "handicraft in the workshops was... not an end in itself, but laboratory experiment preparatory to industrial production"—type-forms or prototypes for a new society, perhaps.[5]

So much for the image of the happy craftsman so fondly imagined by Morris and Ruskin, and Pugin before them! That vision came at a price, both metaphorical and literal. The first involved issues of morality. Take, for example, Pugin's gnomic advice that the architect or craftsman could decorate a construction but should not construct a decoration; or Ruskin's characterisation of painted marbling on wood as an "Architectural Deceit" (and where else in *The Seven Lamps of Architecture* but in the chapter entitled "The Lamp of Truth"?); or Adolf Loos, who famously regarded ornament as crime (yet indulged his shoemaker who took personal pleasure in ornamenting leatherwork with brogue). The actual cost is hinted at in Morris' outburst at his own predicament: "I spend my time ministering to the swinish luxury of the rich."[6] For the Communist radical could do nothing about the labour costs which put his work well beyond any working man's budget—and those costs rose dramatically in the boom of the 1890s, then again between 1914 and 1920 and then again after the Second World War.[7]

Alan Colquhoun summarised the outcome thus:

> ... toward the end of the nineteenth century... new avant-gardes operated between two polar extremes: that of a vitalistic, craft-oriented architecture and that of a rationalistic, machine-oriented architecture.... It was the second strand that became dominant in the post-World War I avant-garde and that set the tone of architectural practice as a whole after World War II.[8]

For that reason modern British architects in the decades after the Second World War were as likely to talk about craft as they were about style (which is to say not very likely at all). There was a dogmatic intolerance of both.

By contrast, decoration made something of a comeback. Perhaps it had never really gone away but simply become a guilty secret that architects denied. Trevor Dannatt, who worked in the London County Council architects' office on the Royal Festival Hall (from 1948 to 1951) in a team lead by Sir Leslie Martin with Peter Moro in charge of the interiors, has recalled that:

> ... we were intent on a richer sort of architecture. There had been an article in *The Architectural Review* about modern decoration or the enrichment of buildings and there might have been an element of that seeping into the Moro consciousness. I'm not sure whether Leslie approved of it or not but we did it and it looked damned good.[9]

And so we have assuredly crafted-looking items such as the cutlery-like bronze and wood inlaid door handles. But we also see bespoke designs for the voluptuous balcony boxes and the carpet pattern with its asymmetrical dot. It is an interior design that marks the building as very unusual in post-war practice but are such bespoke items equivalent to craft? For that matter, is design itself, with all its drawing and model-making, a form of craft? We may quibble with Gregor Eichinger's implication that architects actually make things (as opposed to draw them for other people to make), but we can empathise with his view that "when we as architects produce a surface, it is *we* who are the craftsmen".[10]

The Smithsons may not have cared for the Royal Festival Hall but its overall lightness of touch reflected the optimism of a post-war UK in a way that the 'as-found' could not. Their own view was that "the very heart of present-day architecture [was] the invention of the formal means, whereby, without display or rhetoric, we sense only the essential mechanisms supporting and servicing our buildings.... To make our mechanisms speak with our spaces is our central problem."[11] This is a version of Berlage's attitude at the Amsterdam Exchange (1903), where the decoration arises quasi-naturally through consideration of construction methods such as forming lintols and the spring points for arched brickwork from flush stone dressings or paying unusual attention to everyday necessities such as hoppers and downpipes. The detailing decorates yet the building can be seen as (relatively) unadorned. By way of further examples, consider Louis Kahn's British Gallery at Yale where detailing gives the whole a deep quality that belies its simplicity, or the more overtly decorative use of craft in the work of Carlo Scarpa.[12]

In the last sentence of *Learning from Las Vegas*, Venturi, Scott Brown and Izenour write that "It is now time to re-evaluate the once-horrifying statement of John Ruskin that architecture is the decoration of construction."[13] The authors make this link to Ruskin through their interest in an iconography lost in modernism and by an agreement that architecture is distinguished from building by going beyond what is strictly necessary—by decorating a construction. It was Robert Venturi's iconoclasm in particular that allowed this, introducing a post-functionalist architectural sensibility with the "Gentle Manifesto" that begins his *Complexity and Contradiction in Architecture*.[14] "Gentle" is not quite the word: it is in fact an exhilarating debunking of "the puritanically moral language of orthodox Modern architecture".

However, at least one example of that language should be reabsorbed into our architectural culture. For Louis Sullivan's phrase "form follows function"—such a severe adage!—only became a slogan when removed from its original context. Sullivan's argument, made in 1896, was much more nuanced:

> It is the universal law of everything organic and inorganic, of all things physical and metaphysical, of all things human and superhuman, of all true expressions of head, heart, and soul, that life is to be recognised in its modes of expression, that form always follows function. That is the law.[15]

"Function" for Sullivan is not about use or services or structure and the expression but, as Kees Kaan has argued, about the building's "entire being, character and physiognomy" and its ability to "express intellectual, emotional and spiritual reality".[16]

And it is exactly this richness that Hugh Cullum Architects embrace. It stretches beyond the admittedly fascinating organisations of their buildings to an exceptionally subtle understanding of material qualities and the communicative possibilities that arise from them, their crafting and finishing—and it is not work restricted to expensive materials: there is steel as well as bronze; glass and tile as well as elm and oak. It demonstrates what Richard MacCormac once described as "the intrinsic quality of architecture; its capacity to describe its own making, to root its expressiveness in its own nature as construction joined and proportioned against gravity"—a self-representation that is hard won.[17] Moreover, there is in the Cullum practice's work recurring

evidence that they know about how their buildings will be used, how they will be lived in, how they will change.

With that comes a strong sense that they could have been conceived from the inside out; a sense immediately balanced by their carefully managed relationships to street, garden or court. The external world is particularly evident at the church of St Michael's at Barnes, since the courtyard, or cloister, employed here is such a powerful type. But Hugh Cullum Architects permeate this typology with multiple layers of subtlety. For example, there is its easy engagement with the informal route through the church grounds; then the precise, textured landscaping (designed with BBUK) where the granite-edged floor-scape of porphyry blocks and travertine slabs harmonise with the English bond brickwork and stone of the existing church. Naturally enough, going around corners in English bond demands half-headers to avoid aligned vertical joints, but here, in the brick piers, one senses a particular relish in the pattern. You end up counting: header, half-header, three headers, half-header, header. Just as one looks at the banded brickwork high up on the internal walls of the hall and tries to fathom a sequence from three courses red, one course white, then four red, one white, and alternately three, two, two, three, one, four.... These are simple pleasures, inherent in the material (and surely Ruskin would have approved of the banded courses) but it feels as though we are being shown them afresh and encouraged to look. Familiarity is stimulated by inventiveness. So look at the cloister canopy to see the almost imperceptible rise and fall of the outer face between its supports. These supports double as box gutters which, at the entrance elevation of the hall, discharge rainwater down within their own slender columnar supports to appear near the base through a lipped opening. Then look just above and see the door stops: cylinders of brass with a stainless steel collar. These contrivances, these cosmetic details, designed for daily enjoyment in use, make us ever-so-slightly weak at the knees.

The recently rebuilt jewellery shop on Bond Street is almost literally a jewel box (with hidden compartments beyond the shop floor, too): its double height flush-panelled timber lining incorporates flush bronze-framed display cases; its inlaid marble floor is arranged with mirror patterning;

its magisterial doors, windows, window boxes, awning frames and even an umbrella stand are crafted from solid bronze. Double-sided bronze vitrines, designed like a cross between a Doric temple and its derivative, the Rolls-Royce radiator grill, occupy the windows, showing one side to the street and the other to the shop. Then at the touch of a button a motor swivels them slowly through 180 degrees: the display has become a theatrical device.

The vitrine at a large scale makes the crucial contribution to the artist's studio in Hampstead. Its logical irregularity make the resultant surrounding spaces less predictable both in plan and in section: like a three-dimensional moulding of plaster and glass. The steel handrail to the stairway on the street side of the vitrine gives us the analogy of the painting and the frame, as Hugh has written (and this could be a Ruskinian metaphysical justification, perhaps), moreover its finish of unpainted steel allows it to polish where the visitor rests a hand and to remain dark where less touched, a reminder that Thomas Hardy (an architect and SPAB member as well as a writer) found traditional poetic subjects such as clouds, mists and mountains "unimportant beside the wear on a threshold or the print of a hand".[18] It is good to touch this.

At the Stanley House, a short walk away, Hugh Cullum, in his former practice with Richard Nightingale, made a bricolage using fragments of the site's existing buildings. The result is "like some wonderful, rambling old country house where you are not sure what to expect on opening the door to the next room" as Naomi Stungo wrote in the *RIBA Journal* at the time. The work is mainly new but the haptics suggest otherwise: the second-hand elm boards caulked with oakum and linseed oil before being waxed; the elm spiral staircase with its beautiful assemblage of shaped treads and handsomely connected steel rods. Here again we find pleasure taken in things that move (literally): the secondary stair to the sitting room gallery that pulls up when you wind a handle with a ratchet, its last few treads pivoting up to form a baluster when it comes to rest; the delicate steel framework for the fiddle-back maple of the screen to the spiral stair. The atmosphere is relaxed and accommodating: it is both a cabinet of architectural curiosities and a brilliant meditation on the nature of occupancy and use.

Colin Rowe described this pleasure in the making of things as characteristic of English architecture, "the entrenched English tendency to accentuate every episode and every detail".[19] And it is true to say that if one considers the adjectives one might apply to Hugh Cullum's work—words like quirky, charming, individual, eclectic, kinetic, surprising, Picturesque, characterful, subtle, and humanising—and one puts these together with a light touch, an occasional frisson of the irrational, and an enduring concern to treat each place on its own merit, then you might also have a summary of what Pevsner entitled *The Englishness of English Art*.

Of course, David Watkin alerted us to the confusion in Pevsner's equation of national character with aesthetic character, but as it happens we need not worry.[20] Not only is the work of Hugh Cullum Architects hard to pin down (and all the better for that), but rather inconveniently—at least from the perspective of a writer rounding off an essay—Hugh Cullum is Canadian.

1   Breuer, Marcel, "Architecture and Material", *Circle*, London: Faber and Faber, 1971, p 194.

2   Ryan, Raymund and Iain Sinclair, *The Gritty Brits*. Carnegie Museum of Art, Pittsburgh, 2007.

3   William Morris quoted in a letter to Georgina Burne-Jones, August 1895, in Henderson, Philip, *William Morris his Life, Work and Friends*, London: Thames and Hudson, 1967, p 353.

4   Translated and quoted by Howard Dearstyne in a response to a letter from Gropius in the *Journal of Architectural Education* 18, no 1, June 1963, p 16. I am grateful to Jacqui Goddard for bringing this exchange to my attention.

5   Walter Gropius, letter in *Journal of Architectural Education* 18, no 1, June 1963, p14.

6   Davey, Peter, *Arts and Crafts Architecture*, London: The Architectural Press, 1980, p 27.

7   Powell, CG, *An Economic History of the British Building Industry 1815–1979* London: The Architectural Press, 1980.

8   Colquhoun, Alan, *Modernity and the Classical Tradition*, Cambridge, MA: The MIT Press, 1989, p vii.

9   Dannatt, T, "Subject and Object", *Architectural Research Quarterly*, vol 15, no 1, 2011, p 85.

10 Eichinger, Gregor and Eberhard Tröger, *Touch Me: the Mystery of the Surface*, Baden, Switzerland: Lars Müller Publishers, 2011, pp 27–28.

11 Smithson, Alison and Peter Smithson, *Without Rhetoric—An Architectural Aesthetic*, London: Latimer New Dimensions, 1973, p 14.

12 For further discussion of this aspect of Scarpa's work, see Groak, S, *The Idea of Building*, London: Spon, pp 150–152, and Frampton, Kenneth, "Carlo Scarpa and the Adoration of the Joint", *Studies in Tectonic Culture*, Cambridge, MA: The MIT Press, 1995.

Opposite: Study space in basement flat, Well Mount Studios

13 Venturi, Robert, Denise Scott Brown and Steven Izenour, *Learning from Las Vegas*, Cambridge, MA: The MIT Press, 1977, p 163.

14 Venturi, Robert, *Complexity and Contradiction in Architecture*, London: The Architectural Press, 1977, p 16.

15 Sullivan, Louis H, "The Tall Office Building Artistically Considered", *Sullivan: the Public Papers*, Robert Twombly ed, Chicago: Chicago University Press, 1988.

16 Kaan, Kees "The Choice", *Architectural Research Quarterly*, vol 12, no 2, 2008, p 191.

17 MacCormac, R, "The Pursuit of Quality", *RIBA Journal*, September 1991, p 37.

18 Quoted in Larkin, Philip, *Required Writing*, London: Faber, 1983, p 211.

19 Rowe, Colin, "Eulogy: Jim Stirling", *As I Was Saying*, vol 3, Cambridge, MA: The MIT Press, 1999, p 349.

20 Watkin, D, *Morality and Architecture*, Oxford: Oxford University Press, 1977 pp 78–79.

Above: Courtyard, Well Mount Studios
Overleaf left: Stairs to painting room with rooflight above, Well Mount Studios **Overleaf right:** Print room beyond, Well Mount Studios

Above: Oak-clad bronze column, Heath Street **Opposite:** Street view, Well Mount Studios

Place and Setting

St Michael's Cloister Courtyard and Community Hall

St Michael's Cloister Courtyard and Community Hall

Hugh Cullum

I live in a flat in the Golden Lane Estate, a 1950s precursor to the adjacent Barbican development. I admire the openness and permeability of the public courtyards and the generosity of spirit that led to the inclusion of an on-site tennis court and swimming pool; all accessible from the low-rise flats without having to cross any roads, but without the labyrinthine planning of the later Chamberlain Powell and Bon development at the Barbican. And if you do happen to get lost in the Golden Lane Estate, there are small cast bronze (or are they iron?) relief maps of the estate, mounted, like friend to tell you the way, at key corners of the estate. I've always loved the scale and tactility of these (one day I plan to take a cast of one) and I'd like to think that, like the solid mahogany door and window framing and dado rails within the flats, these are evidence of a thoughtful designer at work, bringing carefully chosen materials and a reassuring sense of longevity to the project.

Every cloistered courtyard design risks creaking under the weight of precedent—there are so many unavoidable exemplars and so relatively few contemporary opportunities to design a cloister courtyard that it almost feels self-indulgent to do so. I am happy to admit though that the relaxed openness of the cloister courtyard at St Michael's was inspired partly by those of the Golden Lane Estate and that the terracotta tile we designed for the frieze was inspired by those cast bronze or iron maps. The terracotta tile is, in a sense, a cipher for the project. It is part of how we see the new work measuring up to the existing building.

St Michael's, designed by Charles Innes in 1893, is fairly typical of the red brick churches erected in the new suburbs of London at the end of the nineteenth century. Although conceived in circumstances of economic austerity (at St Michaels the lack of funds led to the use of two if not three types of not very well-matched bricks for the exterior) the church is not without charm. The exterior has some fancy brickwork and areas of patterned terracotta tiling along with some good quality arts and crafts metalwork and rainwater goods. The interior is like a huge overturned boat. A high space with a wooden ceiling supported on banded brickwork with dressings of glazed wall tiles, encaustic floor mosaic and richly chromatic Victorian stained glass adorning its more sacred parts.

The flat solidity of the enclosing walls, unchallenged by the thin lancet windows, make a dark and mysterious, but very isolated, space—quite unlike the skeletal light-dissolved interior of a Gothic church. Central to the

Opposite: Cloister courtyard, St Michael and All Angels
Previous page: Courtyard wall pinnacle, St Michael and All Angels

mythology of St Michael is his triumph over the forces of darkness and I wonder whether the evocation of this darkness was in the mind of Innes as he sketched out the nave. A similar, though more intense, example of this is experienced at another St Michael, the Sagra di San Michele, at the top of a mountain outside Turin in Northern Italy. Here the sense of dark enclosure is further dramatised by the knowledge that beyond the enclosing walls of the sanctuary is a windy precipitous cliff and a blinding light-soaked vista.

The spatial and spiritual connectedness of these dark spaces is upwards and downwards. They make a point of isolating themselves from their surroundings. Our cloister courtyard, in spite of the name (cloister deriving from *kleisto* or closed), is intended to do quite the opposite.

The south-western edge of the site includes a much-used public right of way connecting Charles Street and Elm Bank Gardens. This was shifted to run across the bottom edge of the courtyard and through the entrance lychgate. Thus the courtyard became a public face of the church off which are the entrances to the church itself, the community hall and the counselling rooms. The constant traffic through the courtyard has meant that the church is not only more visible to the public but that the courtyard has become a popular gathering place. It is rare not to see two or three people smoking or drinking coffee on its benches.

The design of the courtyard changed quite significantly over the ten years or so between our winning the design competition and the start on site. From my days at Sandy Wilson's office, I remember that the design of the British Library also underwent a strange transformation in spirit over its extended design period, in its case from initial conception as a rather sparse Nordic-looking building to something much heavier and more grounded by the time it was built. The massive and rather classicising character of the entrance aedicule, in the south-west corner of the forecourt, sums up the change of spirit.

At an altogether more modest scale, our design for the courtyard had a similar morphosis. What had been a lightweight steel and glass arcade structure around its perimeter became increasingly solid. Timber and steel became stone and brick and the language of shadow gaps and cantilevers, one of an 'assembled' architecture, became more akin to something carved from a solid. I guess this was partly owed to the spirit of the times. Postmodern fantasies were popping up faster than you could press the mirror duplicate button on your drawing programme. But it was also a realisation that a closer dialogue with Innes' church could be had by moving a bit closer to its materials and mode of expression.

Also, there were those on the building committee who were deeply unhappy with our initial proposals for a courtyard architecture that "looked like a bus shelter" and I had to admit that, certainly as far as the perception

Top: Cast plaque, Golden Lane Estate **Bottom:** Sagra di San Michele, Turin **Opposite:** Community hall, St Michael and All Angels

46

of the general public was concerned, they had a point. In addition, practical considerations, such as the shelter and degree of visual screening offered by the cloister and the discouragement of vandalism, all pushed in the direction of a more solid construction.

With the adoption of stone and brick came a more crafted approach to the detailing. The tall stone backs to the benches (inspired by the benches at Barons Court tube station) turned forward at the top to provide rain hoods. The stone was beautifully tapered and shaped to deflect the weather and provide a comfortable anthropomorphic sitting surface.

Where there had been extensive glass roofing in the initial design there was now a lead-clad timber roof with glass at intervals, allowing light to punctuate the benches under tiny stone-roofed pinnacles. The lychgate had become a more recognisably typical structure of heavy oak members with a curved boarded roof, reminiscent of the nave of Innes' church.

It had become a complicated construction and we made several large-scale models in developing the details alongside a wonderfully talented and understanding builder, David Lightfoot, whose three-dimensional construction sketches are an object lesson to any architect.

Because the fees had long since dried up, the project became a labour of love, not only for me and for the generations of colleagues who worked on it, but also for the client—the parish building committee, led by Peter Howe, and the two or three vicars over whose tenure the project spanned. It was Peter who shepherded the project through the financial obstructions, the virulent nimbyish local opposition (leading to a consistorial court hearing) and the wayward aesthetic prejudices of the committee, to its eventual completion. In particular, he was a champion of practical, long-lived construction and the use of (sometimes expensive) high-quality materials. He often said that we should be designing a building with a lifespan of at least a hundred years.

Although it was built as the first phase, the hall was the third term in its relationship to the church and courtyard. Four brick piers establish the corners of the hall space and between them is slung a white folded ceiling, rather as a cloth might be suspended between four trees. The ceiling stops short of the edges to allow a diffuse light to wash down the side walls. Like many such halls, it had to be suitable for a range of purposes. As a space for events, like wedding receptions, it was seen as an adjunct to the courtyard with an openable glass facade onto it. Blinds and acoustic curtains allow it to work equally well for yoga classes, as a nursery space or for rehearsals and small concerts. Behind are the servant spaces of the kitchen, WCs and a flower-arranging room.

The hall is set a couple of metres off the exterior side wall of the nave, giving a gap which absorbs the ins and outs of the external wall and provides

Opposite: Cloister stone benches, St Michael and All Angels

and interstitial circulation space. From this we made a large new opening into the nave of the church and it is here that the vicar shakes hands with the congregation as they file out after a service to take coffee in the new hall. In the same space the choir assembles before processing through the new door into the nave.

It was important that the four new piers, replete with niches for their absent apostles, were made of the same stuff as the original church. We had a brick company revive their Victorian brick press to produce a special "St Michael's mix", which we used for the hall and cloister with the patterned terracotta tiles and Portland stone.

Returning finally to the terracotta tile. It represents, as you might have guessed, a plan of the church and courtyard. The courtyard is represented as a circular gathering space, a singular event, and the church, with the font at one end and altar at the other, as a repetitive communion. The gently sloping planes within the circle play with light and shade to recall the enveloping cloak of St Michael as he vanquishes the darkness below him.

Above: Terracotta frieze tile, St Michael and All Angels
Opposite: Carved Portland lettering, St Michael and All Angels

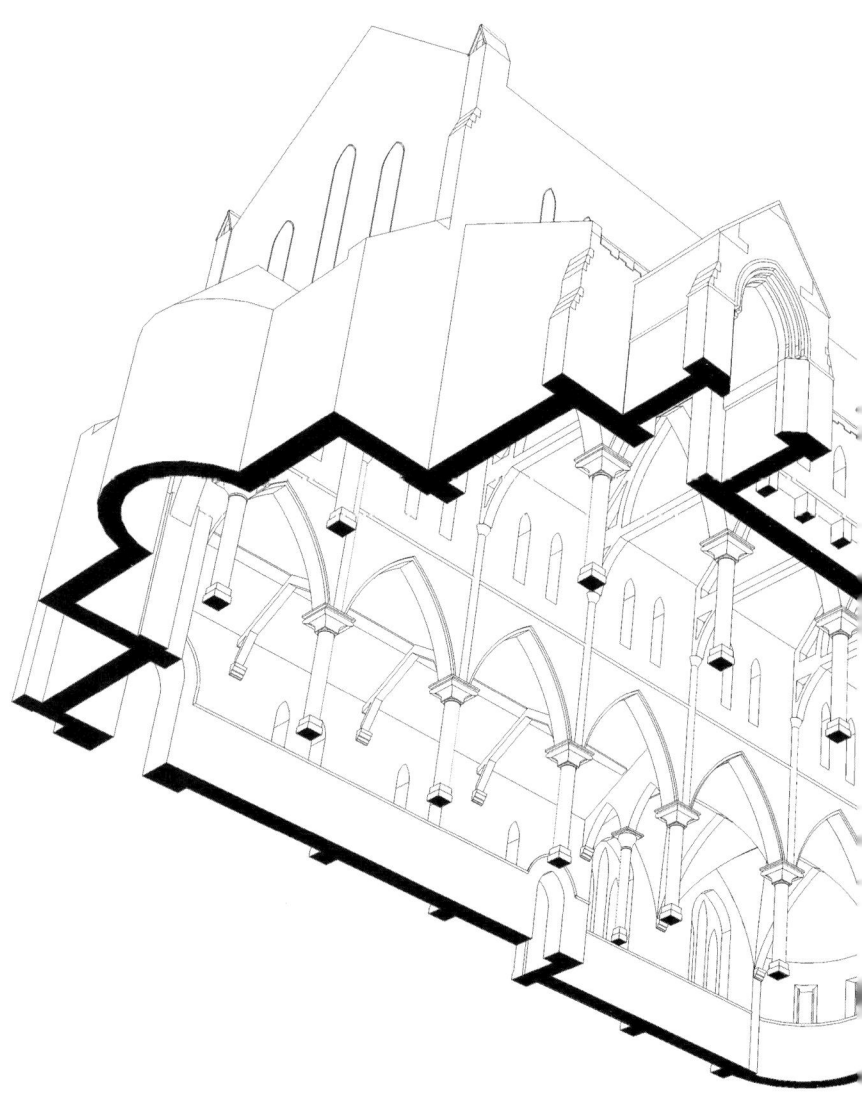

Up-view after Choisy, St Michael and All Angels

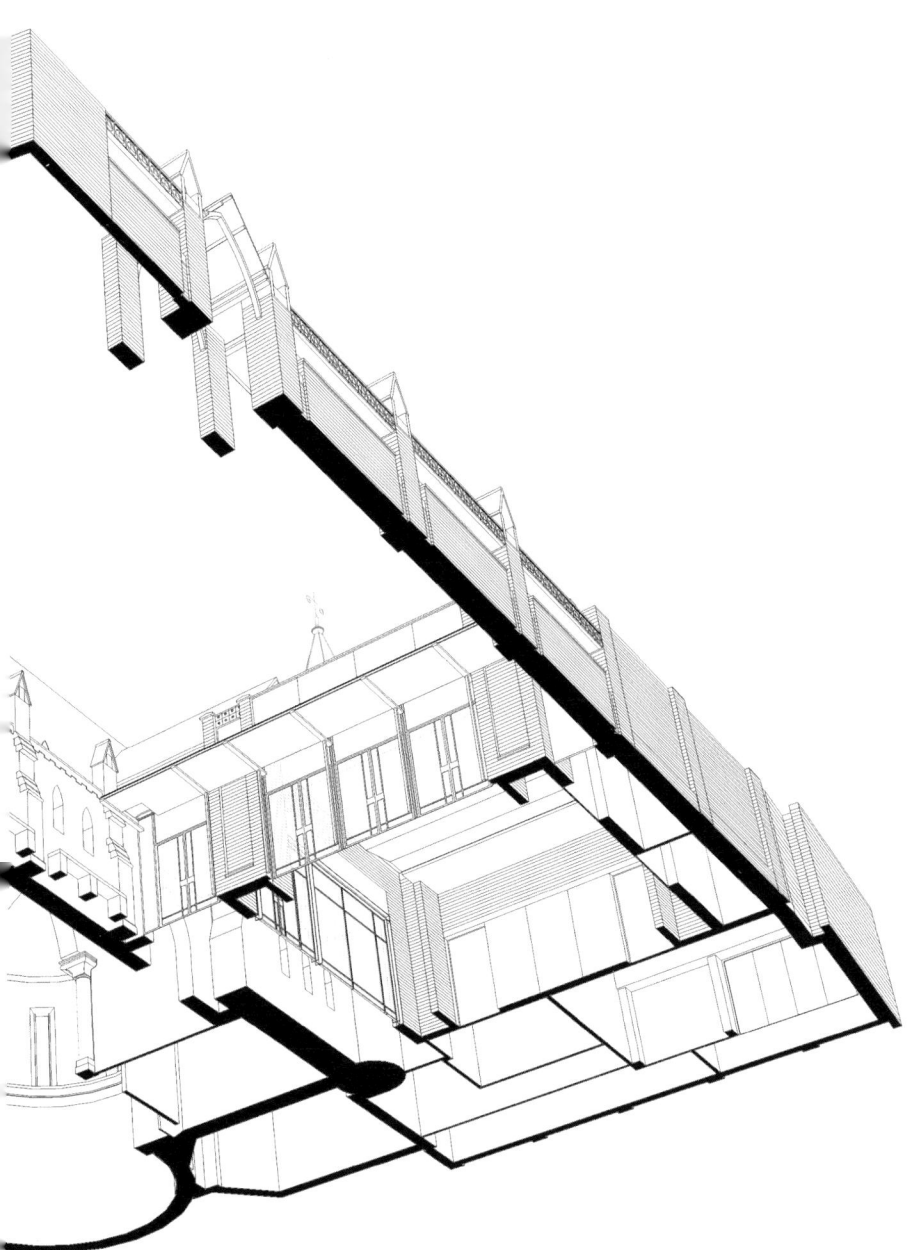

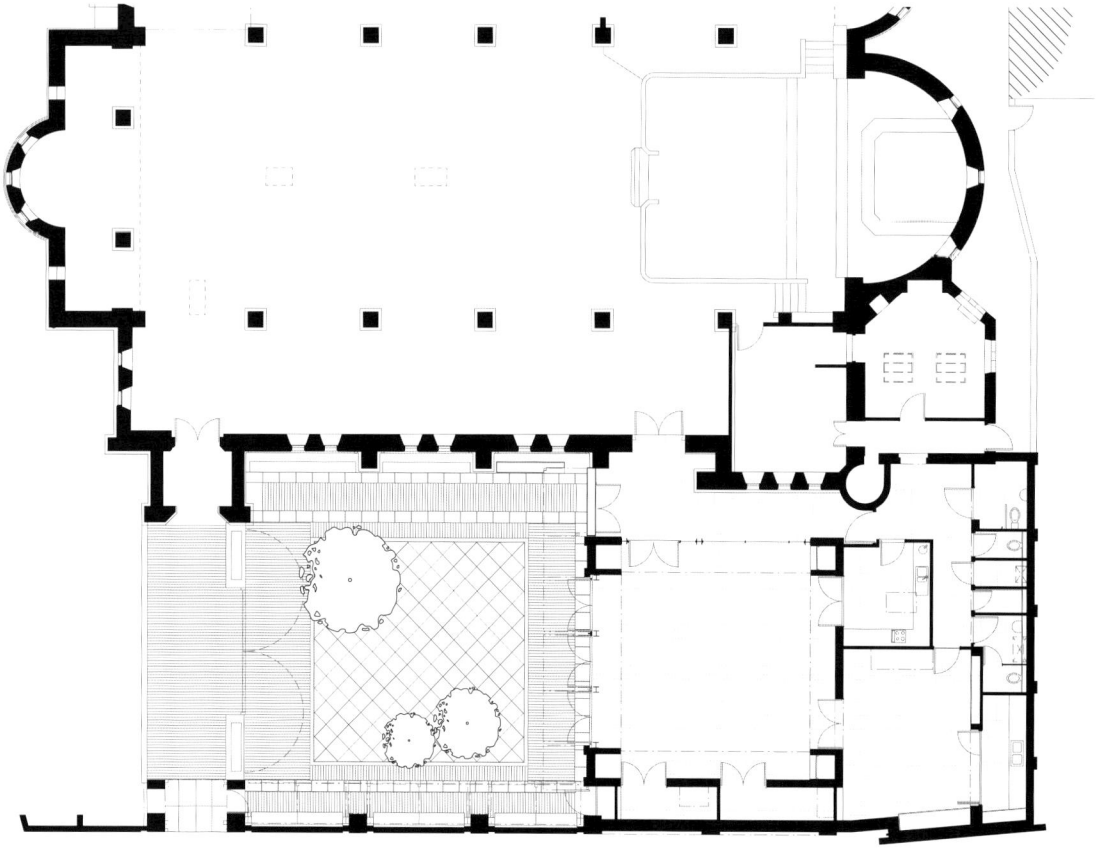

Plan of new hall and courtyard, St Michael and All Angels

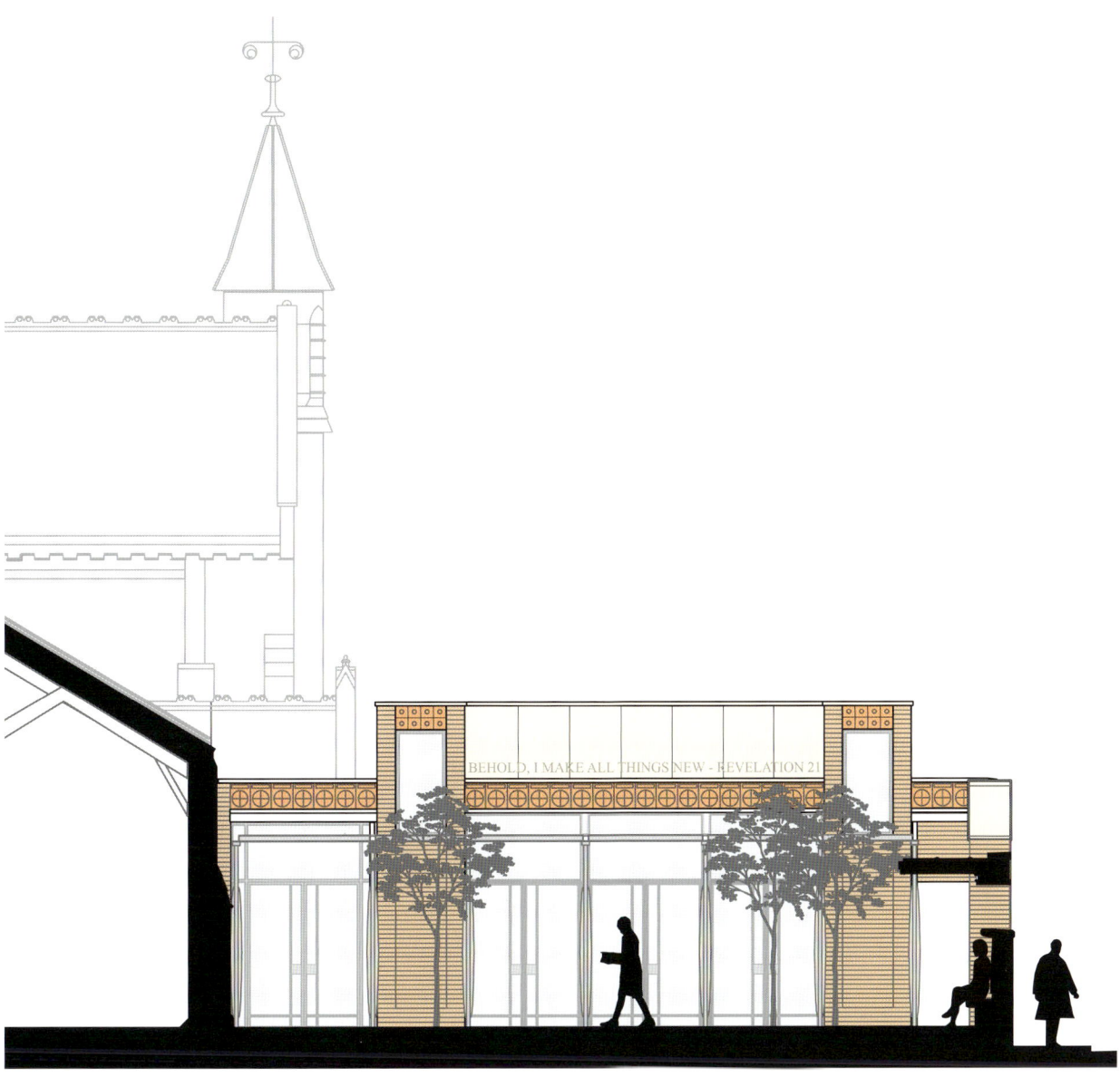

BEHOLD, I MAKE ALL THINGS NEW - REVELATION 21

Entrance elevation of hall, St Michael and All Angels

Elevation to Cross Street, St Michael and All Angels

St Michael's, Barnes: Place and Setting

Alan Powers

It is a commonplace of planning administration in England that a new building should be 'in keeping' with its neighbours and surroundings. What, one might ask, is wrong about that? Hasn't modern architecture done enough damage in the past through insensitivity of scale and materials? The trouble is that someone has to decide what this character consists of, and then decide how to interpret it in the wordless medium of architecture.

Modernist architecture has often been defined in terms of its technological and social imperatives. According to this view, it should stand by its own logic and not be required to reflect the manners or material of the past, since such disguises will never be convincing. In the past, it has been argued, new buildings that we now insist on preserving were similarly shocking as they forged the path of the future. The difficulty with arguments on both sides is that while some architects are good enough to break the rules and justify the disturbance they cause, others are not. Architecture being the public art that it is, such issues are important, but if the judgment of buildings that already exist is hard to objectify, then how much more difficult it will be for buildings yet to be constructed.

Thankfully, some of the best architects of the past 30 years have set themselves the task of working in a sympathetic way alongside interesting and good buildings and finding ways of gaining strength in their design from the conversation that takes place. Technology and society need not be denied their proper place in the transformation, but neither is the field a completely clear one—indeed, with the planning system based on the views of elected councillors in local authorities, it is never likely to be, since these decision-makers may vote according to their own views, aligning these to what they think their constituents want. Hugh Cullum writes that his scheme, while supported by the vicar and the parish building committee, "didn't endear us to the planners or certain sections of the local community who would probably have preferred to see something with a few more pitched roofs and gothic arches".

The addition by Hugh Cullum Architects at St Michael's, Barnes, is an outstandingly successful example of having a conversation with a neighbour in architectural terms. The neighbour, in this case, is a rather noble Victorian red-brick church that, on its consecration in 1893, would have seemed architecturally 40 years behind the times. By the 1890s, church design had tended to become more refined and sometimes more ornamental, but here we find the plain brick walls and paired lancet windows of the "vigorous style" that has sometimes been seen as a distant precursor of Modernism, with its truth to materials and simplification of form. The church was, rather belatedly, listed during the course of the project. Hugh writes about how the "admirable simplicity and honesty [and] the unadorned materials give it a formidable presence".

Seeing the Community Hall and its courtyard on the south side of the church today, it is hard to believe that there was formerly only a much smaller choir room dating from the 1930s, standing at the back of a scruffy piece of grass. In the process of transformation, the enclosed spaces of the Community Centre are balanced by the open space of the courtyard, and linked by the boundary wall and gateway to make a grouping with consistent materials, dimensions and thinking. One hopes that those who objected at the planning stage can now see the point of designing this way, and are gratified by the concession of open stone 'pinnacles' sitting on the piers of the wall with their roll mouldings at the peak that bring back an echo of Gothic.

The planning requirements of the Community Centre are relatively simple, involving two spaces—a hall and a much smaller choir room. Around these are distributed the "servant" spaces, loos, cupboards etc. When the larger and smaller spaces are seen together on the plan, we find that it is an example of a "tartan grid", one of the planning principles current in the Cambridge School of Architecture when Hugh was a student. As with a tartan fabric, there are intersecting narrow bands (the non-architect must imagine dotted lines in some cases to join them up) that fall at regular intervals across the background surface. These little spaces, marked out by pillars or solid chunks of wall can best be sensed by

Opposite: View through lychgate, St Michael and All Angels

standing in the middle of the hall, where there is one in each corner, making doorways in the inner wall and intriguing niches towards the courtyard where you can sit and let the light fall from above. Spanning between east and west along the tartan lines are high runs of clerestory windows, producing one of architecture's time-honoured and seldom-failing special effects, the hidden light source. When sunlight pours down the new wall, echoing the Ruskinian fabric of the original church with its banding of brick and stone, casting angled shadows from the unseen glazing bars above, the effect is delightful as light and dark stripes intersect, becoming more predominantly white as they rise up to the light.

The generous cupboard spaces off the closed side of the hall are lower than the central section, which rises up as a square lantern from its base between the four brick corners. This line of the tartan grid extends into the covered way along the wall to the gateway, and is balanced by the parallel corridor to the north, which is separated from the hall by a glass partition. In reality, this is all simpler and more natural than the complicated words that are needed to describe it, but none the less clever for that.

The sense of being indoors in a particular rather than a generic space is enhanced by the attention to the profiling of the ceilings in both the rooms. The ceiling in the choir room gives it character, dropping down between two sources of daylight at each end and providing recesses for the electric lighting. In the hall, the ceiling also bends down towards the middle, although slightly off centre.

The sense of sitting comfortably (the question asked at the beginning of the old Home Service *Children's Hour* on the BBC) is especially well answered in the stone bench seats that back onto the courtyard wall. Without visiting the site, it is hard to see the way this wall not only does the usual things that walls do, but works as part of the street picture and is connected to a longer wall along the narrow pedestrian Thorne Passage that runs eastwards. It is one of those features of suburbs that crop up to provide not only a handy short cut but a sense of mystery of the kind so well depicted in the paintings of the Royal Academician Carel Weight, based on nearby riverine Putney. There are three seats in a row, each broad enough for a pair or threesome, looking in towards the chequerboard paving of the courtyard, its stur-

dy gates, the two trees and the planting along the base of the Victorian aisle. The stone seats and their high backs are well judged to the needs of the body but, just as important, there are gaps where the back wall dips down next to the piers, perfect for peeking out into the world beyond. These seats exemplify what is called the "prospect-refuge" theory of architecture and landscape which, if impossible to prove from historical evidence, is convincing according to the test of experience. Early mankind, the theory goes, living in the savannahs of northern Africa, would have valued a place to sit in the shade, perhaps under a tree, with something solid to his back, a good view to the front, and the chance to see all round without being seen. Thus predators could be evaded and hunting opportunities taken. So, the seats are not only a comfort to the body but also to the soul.

The sense of a cloistered courtyard is gently reinforced by the canopy that projects in front of the three pairs of French doors connecting the hall to the courtyard. Practical, certainly, in terms of extending the space on a wet day— imagine guests at a wedding craning their necks from here to see the cake being cut inside—but also a useful baffle if the afternoon light beats too strongly on the glass. In the psychic realm, the underside of the canopy, low enough to reach up and touch, marks a transitional space between inside and out. The steel supports are made warm to the touch by cambered strips of wood screwed onto them. Rainwater runs down the hollow centres. The precise square shape of the courtyard is defined on the fourth side by low iron grilles with wide-opening gates in the centre, fastened by a satisfyingly chunky brass bolt with its reeded knobs.

The gate from the road, reminiscent of a country lychgate, is the last in the collection of characters that make up this drama. It is important in part because a public footpath crosses the churchyard at the west end, another useful short cut among the long streets of houses. With trees fringing the boundary, the path gives the illusion of being in the country and people make it part of their everyday lives, popping out round the apsed west wall to emerge into the light of the courtyard.

There is restraint as well as richness in the choice of materials for this project. Brick takes the lead and defines inside and outside, and what bricks they are. Well matched to their Victorian neighbours with a slightly glazed surface, the bricks have more variety of colour and are beautifully laid and pointed in the special "St Michael's mix" of mortar, with white joints wider than the Victorians would have used. Good pointing is rare and few architects or building owners appreciate how it has the capacity to lift the experience of a building from the ordinary to the special, like adding the right amount of salt in cookery, providing a pervasive but not intrusive enhancement to what appears to be the main ingredient. Matched to the brick, although differing in colour and surface texture, are the panels of moulded or plain terracotta that provide decoration, a surface for the play of shadow and a rhythmic procession along a continuous band above the bays of seating and over what one is tempted to call the portico leading into the hall.

Comparing the materials and workmanship at Barnes with those of the British Library is a revealing exercise. The more recent building marks an upward shift in sensitivity, not so much progress as a beneficial regression to an earlier and better condition. All credit to David Lightfoot and the builders at Barnes for such an impeccable job in a project that works hard in the invisible areas to make things look so easy.

In relation to the theme of place-making, it would be hard to find a better example of intervening in an already crowded corner of a city and weaving everything together so that the whole becomes so much greater than the sum of the parts, but in saying this, one acknowledges that the newcomer to the party is actually the belle of the ball. It achieves something like the effect of the Pazzi Chapel, added in the 1440s to the south side of the great Florentine Gothic church of Santa Croce, nearly 200 years after the start of the parent building. The Pazzi Chapel is noted for its self-sufficient achievement in pure Renaissance architecture, with its open loggia and internal dome, tiny but exquisite alongside the great bulk of the main basilica. The sense of space created in the angle between the two buildings, with a direct axial path leading to the entrance, is in both cases a major part of the attraction, but dare one say that with its smaller scale and its many signs of inhabitation, Barnes stands fair to beat Florence.

The reference to Florence is quite unconscious on Hugh's part, it seems, but it is perhaps not surprising that his

sensibility should be set on the Renaissance. This is not just because most architecture students do the round of Italian sites sooner or later, but rather because Hugh's teacher at Cambridge and later employer, Colin St John Wilson, was obsessed the writings of Adrian Stokes (1902–1972), who studied the period in a very personal way in his books, *The Quattro Cento*, 1932 and *Stones of Rimini*, 1934. Cambridge students were invited by Wilson to pick copies of Stokes's books out of a box and take them away. Many of the most inviting aspects of the British Library on which Hugh worked for Wilson and his large and close-knit team of designers in the 1980s, can be traced back to Stokes's writings, which pre-empted by 50 years the phenomenological trend in architectural criticism and theory.

Put simplistically, phenomenology is a way of describing or thinking about the feeling of belonging in a place that we can experience intuitively, but which is hard to put into words. Phenomenology deals with the combination of all the senses, not just the visual, with which architecture is mainly associated. Light, shade, temperature, humidity, sound and smell are all involved, as well as the effect of passing between different zones of these. Wilson's whole outlook was revolutionised when he first heard the Norwegian champion of phenomenology in architecture, Christian Norberg-Schultz, speaking at the RIBA in the 1960s. During the years that followed, it became clear that many other architects across the world were simultaneously rebelling against the mechanistic assumptions that had clustered around modernism between the wars and persisted as a justification for concentrating on production output rather than intangible qualities thereafter. As Hugh describes in his text on Barnes, there was a slow transformation in the British Library design, a kind of warming-up process as some of the implications of monumentality came to be accepted for this unavoidably monumental project, while the chilling qualities associated with this word were humanised by attention to small details and tactile surfaces.

At the British Library, features that might be considered secondary characteristics became primary ones on account of the sympathetic emotions that they can invoke. The broad squares of marble and brick in the square outside encourage you to linger, whether you are a reader or a passer-by looking for peace and quiet under the sky off Euston Road. The intimate but formal circular space, with brick piers topped by carved stones by Stephen Cox, was one of Hugh's responsibilities as part of the team, and it is not hard to find echoes of it at Barnes. If you can bear to leave the Library courtyard on a sunny day, you go through the low entrance doors and into the expansive space that seems like a different outdoors. Around the edges are a few stone seats built into niches, which, even if you don't choose to sit in them, convey a comforting idea of sitting. Stone balustrades demarcate zones across another chequerboard floor where today, unanticipated by their creator, students from across the world sit pensively at their laptops. The attraction of these spaces for silent but communal study is solid proof of putting theory successfully into practice. The curves which the young Hugh slyly inserted into one of the design models of the lofty ceiling and which were gratefully accepted by the master, make their contribution too.

Adrian Stokes wrote in *The Quattro Cento* that the South, that condition of light and culture to which he attributed the unique spiritual qualities of the Renaissance, was a place "in which life is outward, spread in space". Many architects now aspire to create these qualities in buildings that feel right to their users without any need for gimmicks. The addition at Barnes uses a combination of devices to spread life outward in space. The transparency of the big room contributes, yet this is balanced by the inwardness of the hidden light sources and the aedicules (literally, little houses) formed by the brick piers of the tartan grid. (It was a contemporary of Adrian Stokes, a better-known architectural historian, John Summerson, under a strong influence of the psychologist CJ Jung, who argued in his essay "Heavenly Mansions" that aedicules were one of the basic elements of architecture.)

More obviously, it is the way that the inside-outside relationship at Barnes is developed that contributes to its achievement of poetic dwelling. The flowering shrubs and the trees contribute their softness and their light-gathering qualities, casting shadows on the floor of brick and stone, as well as scents and reminders of the passage of the seasons. The courtyard clearly works in relation to the building and its interiors, but it is tempting to say that it is the most successful part of the whole project, if only because outdoor spaces seldom get treated with this level of care and thoughtfulness. The space is full of incident but avoids the well-intentioned clutter of planters, sculpture and scattered furniture that reduces public space to a forlorn version of a private garden. It is even rather a blessing that the quotation for the *Book of Revelations*, "Behold I make all things new", is so inconspicuous above the canopy in front of the hall. It is nice to be reminded, but the building already says it, although it is not so much things as relationships of space and substance that have been made new here.

Lychgate, St Michael and All Angels

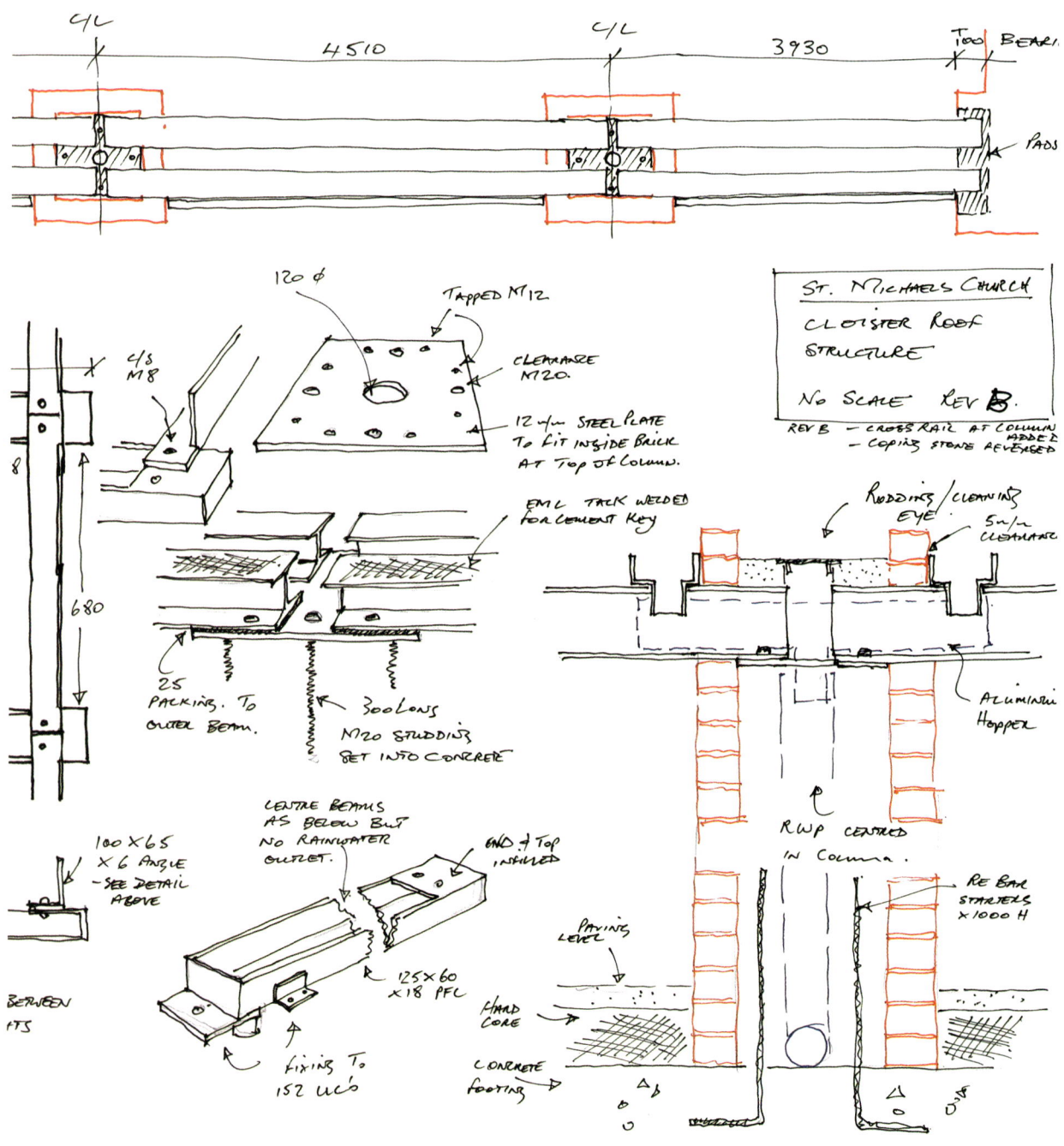

ST. MICHAELS CHURCH
CLOISTER ROOF
STRUCTURE

NO SCALE   REV B.

REV B - CROSS RAIL AT COLUMN
        ADDED
      - COPING STONE REVERSED

4510   3930

C/L   C/L   100 BEAM

PADS

120 ∅   TAPPED M12

CLEARANCE
M20.

12 m/m STEEL PLATE
To FIT INSIDE BRICK
AT TOP OF COLUMN.

C/S
M8

8

680

EML TACK WELDED
FOR CEMENT KEY

25
PACKING. TO
OUTER BEAM.

300 LONG
M20 STUDDING
SET INTO CONCRETE

RODDING / CLEANING
EYE   5m/m
CLEARANCE

ALUMINIUM
HOPPER

RWP CENTRED
IN COLUMN.

100 × 65
× 6 ANGLE
~ SEE DETAIL
ABOVE

BETWEEN
FTS

CENTRE BEAMS
AS BELOW BUT
NO RAINWATER
OUTLET.

END & TOP
INSTALLED

125 × 60
× 18 PFC

FIXING TO
152 UC'S

PAVING
LEVEL

HARD
CORE

CONCRETE
FOOTING

RE BAR
STARTERS
× 1000 H

Above: Contractor's construction sketches, St Michael and All Angels **Opposite:** Courtyard exterior wall, St Michael and All Angels

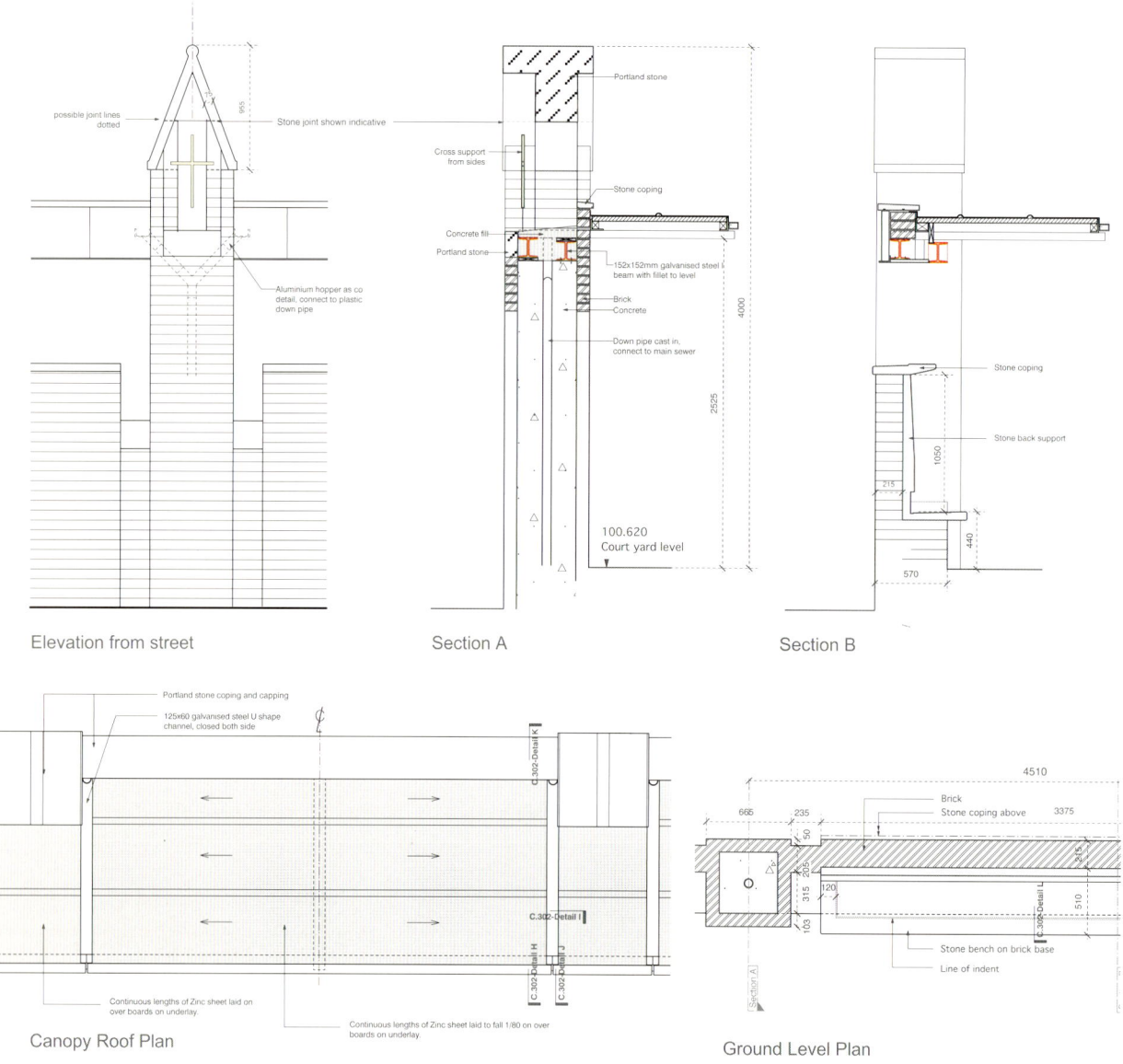

Elevation from street

possible joint lines dotted

Stone joint shown indicative

Aluminium hopper as co detail, connect to plastic down pipe

Section A

Portland stone

Cross support from sides

Stone coping

Concrete fill

Portland stone

152x152mm galvanised steel beam with fillet to level

Brick

Concrete

Down pipe cast in, connect to main sewer

4000

2525

100.620
Court yard level

Section B

Stone coping

Stone back support

1050

215

440

570

Canopy Roof Plan

Portland stone coping and capping

125x60 galvanised steel U shape channel, closed both side

C.302-Detail K

C.302-Detail H

C.302-Detail I

C.302-Detail J

Continuous lengths of Zinc sheet laid on over boards on underlay.

Continuous lengths of Zinc sheet laid to fall 1/80 on over boards on underlay.

Ground Level Plan

4510

665   235   3375

50

205

315   120

103   510

315

Brick

Stone coping above

Stone bench on brick base

Line of indent

Section A

C.302-Detail L

Above: Pinnacle construction drawing, St Michael and All Angels **Opposite:** Lychgate detail, St Michael and All Angels
Overleaf left: Entrance canopy, St Michael and All Angels **Overleaf right:** Coffee after the service, St Michael and All Angels

Perspective drawing, St Michael and All Angels

Meaning and Metaphor

Pavilion Landscape House

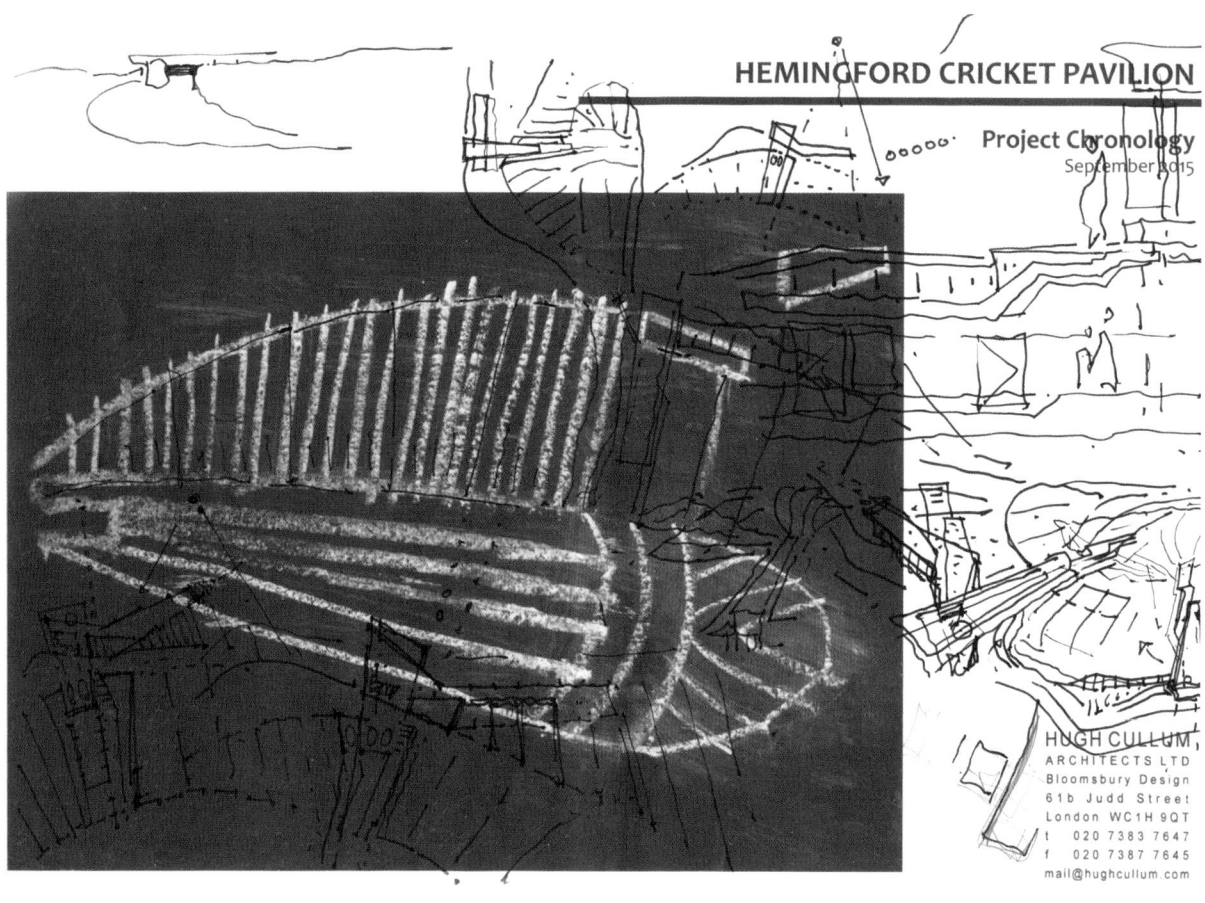

HEMINGFORD CRICKET PAVILION

Project Chronology
September 2015

HUGH CULLUM,
ARCHITECTS LTD
Bloomsbury Design
61b Judd Street
London WC1H 9QT
t 020 7383 7647
f 020 7387 7645
mail@hughcullum.com

Above: Report cover with Whiteford's sketch and our pentimenti, Pavilion Landscape House
Previous Page: Site model, Pavilion Landscape House

Pavilion Landscape House

Hugh Cullum

Occasionally separate events come together to present unexpected opportunities and this commission is one of these. We have been working on a contemporary walled garden and pool house in the grounds of a manor house by Decimus Burton (see later chapter). Unfortunately the original manor house estate was broken up at the beginning of the twentieth century and its thatched and half-timbered cricket pavilion was sold off on a separate parcel of land. We were therefore especially excited when the current owners of the pavilion asked for our help in developing a strategy for restoring it and building a new house. It gave us the opportunity to address (or perhaps redress) the separation of manor house and pavilion and to metaphorically reconnect the two by working with the theme of the country house landscape.

This exciting commission of the Cricket Pavilion and Landscape House is a work of collaboration between Hugh Cullum Architects and the artist Kate Whiteford OBE. The work is still in progress and the drawings here present a snapshot of where we are now.

The listed cricket pavilion was built in 1897 as part of the neighbouring manor house estate, designed by Decimus Burton and dating from 1843. It was conceived as a *cottage orné* with a veranda overlooking the cricket pitch and first-floor accommodation for the visiting professional cricketers, who would be employed to come and play the gentlemen staying in the main house.

In the twentieth century the pavilion was sold off, resulting in adjustment of the estate's boundary so that it scraped by just in front of the pavilion, thereby separating it from its historic context. Even now, although the pavilion is no longer in the ownership of the main house, Burton's four-square building remains a visible presence in the distance, glimpsed through established trees. Although the pavilion itself is historically associated with the manor house estate, most of the current site has never been within its curtilage but was agricultural land to the edge of Hemingford Abbots and became a hinterland between the village and the estate at its creation in the 1840s.

The client had a history of unsuccessful attempts to further extend the cricket pavilion (which had already been extended several times) and asked us to look afresh at the problem. The motive was not so much the need for more space as for a more practical and workable arrangement of rooms.

We made a number of exploratory proposals for demolishing the existing extensions and adding a single coherent new one. However, to match the size of the existing accommodation, these schemes were fairly large and still imposed unsatisfactorily on the original thatched pavilion. As a result, it was agreed that we should be much more modest in the extension and perhaps put some of it underground in an attempt to declutter the pavilion and allow it to be seen properly as an (almost) free-standing symmetrical piece. To compensate for the reduction in accommodation we would design an additional new house elsewhere on the site at some distance from the pavilion.

The site lies just outside the village boundary of Hemingford Abbots and so, while it is well related to the village, it is also in the open countryside. Government guidance resists isolated homes in the countryside. The only path around the legislation is allowed in paragraph 55 of the National Planning Policy Framework—famous as the creation of a past minister who was concerned to "keep alive" the English tradition of building grand country houses on large estates. This curious piece of legislation stipulates that such houses must be of exceptional design quality or of an innovative nature and sets the tests that their design should:

· be truly outstanding or innovative, helping to raise standards of design more generally in rural areas;
· reflect the highest standards in architecture;
· significantly enhance its immediate setting; and
· be sensitive to the defining characteristics of the local area.

Paragraph 55 has indeed spawned some interesting houses, many of them underground or environmentally highly innovative. Usually their suitability for planning permission is not judged directly by the local council but by a design review panel, made up of independent architects, planners, etc, of significant repute.

We were aware that it would be a particular challenge to satisfy the paragraph 55 criteria. Generally our projects are not 'innovative' in a headline-grabbing sort of way, nor are they overtly technologically sophisticated.

The pavilion is sited on the flat and rather featureless flood plain of the River Ouse. I have always had an interest in manipulation of landscape and, given the artificial landscape of the adjacent manor house with its rolling terrain and ponds, very much after the style of Capability Brown, it seemed highly appropriate to create a sympathetically manipulated landscape here.

This gave us the idea of producing something that was part landscape and part architecture and that meant there had to be a collaboration between us and a landscape artist or architect. We needed a Capability Brown. I had worked with Kate Whiteford previously on the British High Commission in Kenya and was fascinated by her large-scale landscape art and interpretation of site history and archaeology. It seemed an ideal opportunity to

Above: Thatched cricket pavilion, Pavilion Landscape House **Opposite:** Whiteford's concept sketches, Pavilion Landscape House

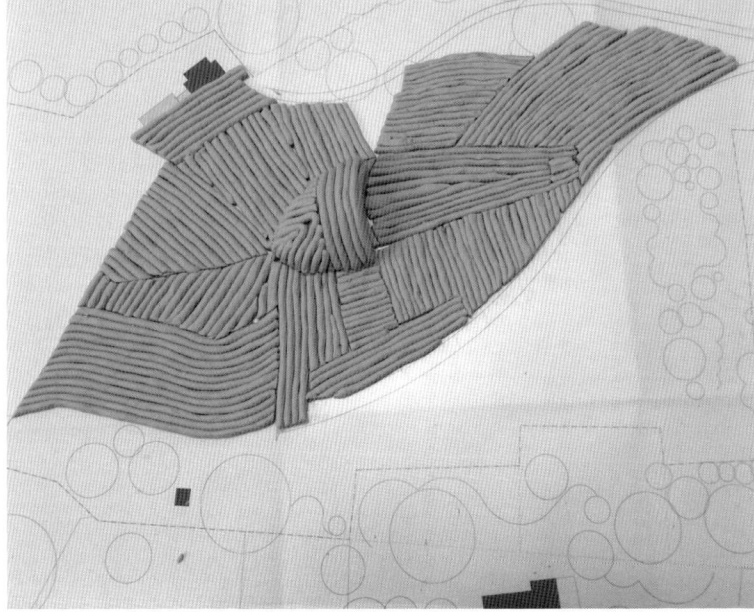

Top: Modelling table with construction lines to manor house, Pavilion Landscape House
Bottom: Whiteford's clay site model showing ridge and furrow, Pavilion Landscape House

team up with her to create something extraordinary and original and she very kindly agreed to be the other half of the design team. Entirely by coincidence and unknown to me, she had worked in a Capability Brown landscape at Harewood House and was about to have an exhibition—False Perspectives (at The Mercer Gallery in Harrogate)—which explored Brown's influence on her work. This echoed my own interest in the perspectival games played in the great continental gardens of the Baroque.

Whiteford's work grows out of the landscape in which it is situated by making reference to the archaeology and the topography of the site. She often makes monumental land drawings that reflect a hidden narrative and reveal another aspect to the site. In each work the irony and play of ideas is underscored by the clever manipulation of the drawing, which has the correct perspective from a given 'viewing point', while, if seen from above, it may be almost unrecognisable.

In our work with Whiteford at Hemingford there is an extensive intervention across the whole site, creating an almost padded landscape out of which Whiteford's focal image of a cricket pad grows by stealth. The 'padding', a reference to ridge and furrow agriculture (the remnants of which is can still be detected on the estate), evokes an era before the Act of Enclosure when the land was farmed by smallholders. The smallholdings were later subsumed by the larger estates, like that at Hemingford, and with them came the leisured classes who had the time and money to indulge in pastimes such as country house cricket.

The development of the 'padded landscape' is one of a number of multi-layered references which underpin the treatment of site and building. This is recognised by Yves Abrioux (in an unpublished essay of 2015) who aptly describes Whiteford's work at Hemingford as "textural archaeology".

We began work with Whiteford on a number of card site models for the new house and landscape, exploring how the new work should relate to the existing cricket pavilion. Whiteford did a series of sketches and together we worked on the idea of some kind of earth sculpture that would 'situate' the house and onto which Whiteford's land-drawing would be projected.

From the outset, the idea of the house was part of our thinking about the land art. Whiteford brought a rich range of images to the project relating to themes of agricultural archaeology, to English landscape garden history, to cricket, and to life in a country house.

Her sketches of bird-like shapes and cricket paraphernalia writ large in the landscape always had 'hard bits' corresponding, for example, to beaks and claws amongst a field of feathers or perhaps intricacies of detail in a cricket pad whose differentiation could develop into some sort of building structure. The development of the scheme was an exciting collaboration. We traded rough models on which Whiteford would draw with brush or chalk. We would

Above: Whiteford's Chippendale Sofa at Harewood House **Overleaf:** Site development models, Pavilion Landscape House

81

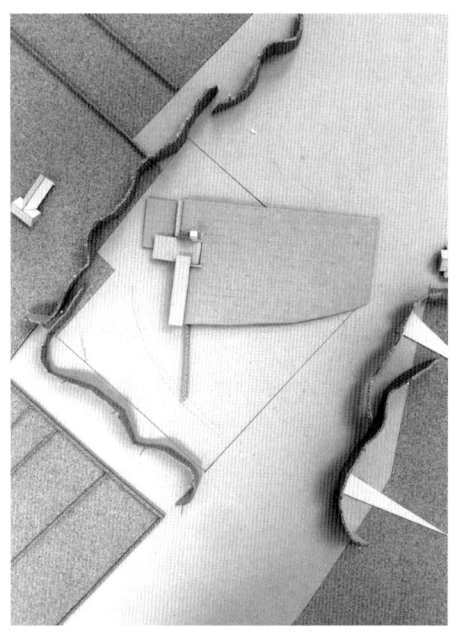

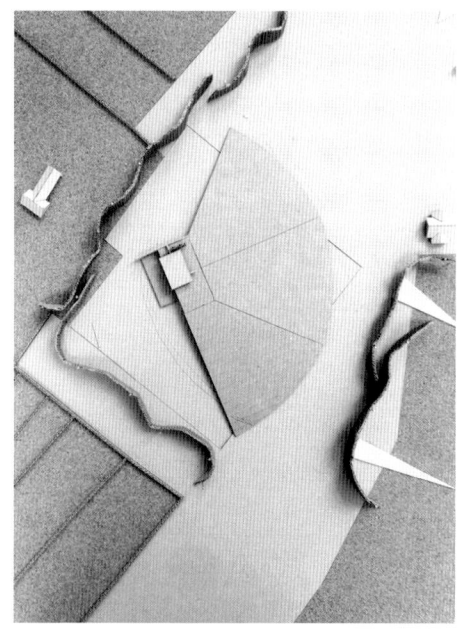

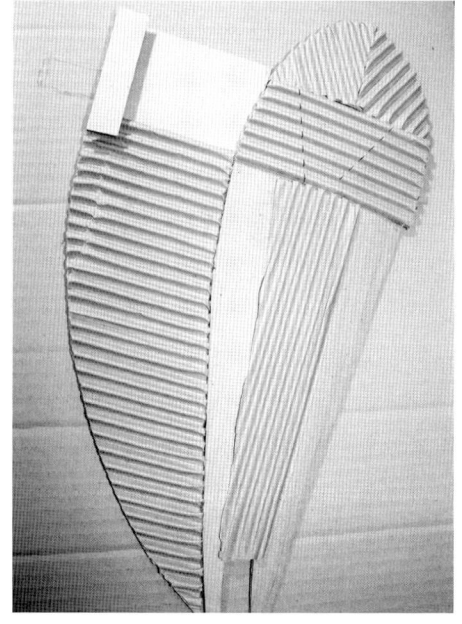

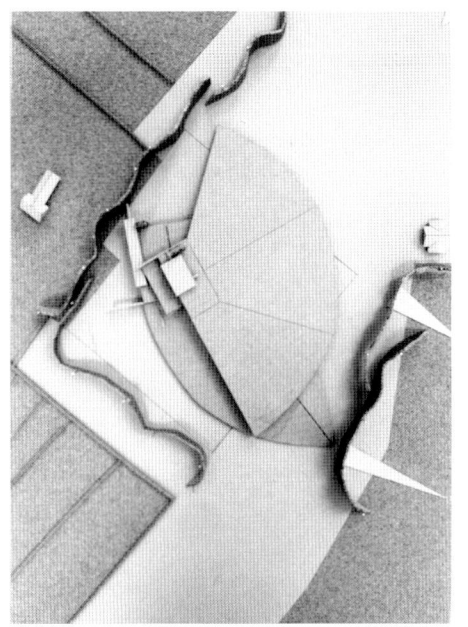
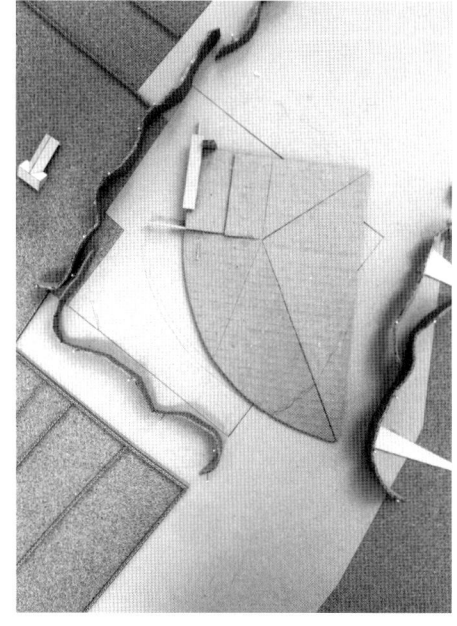
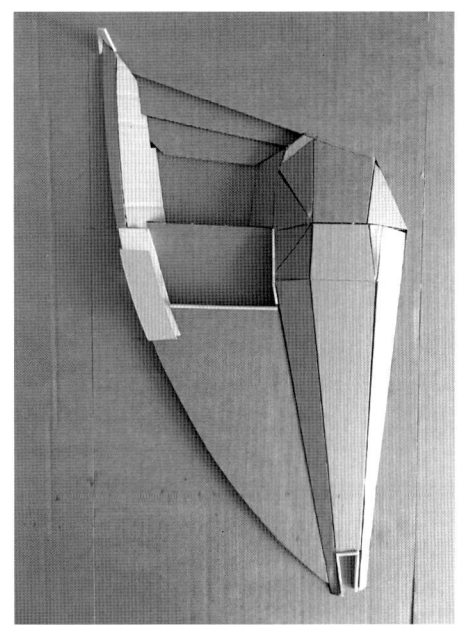
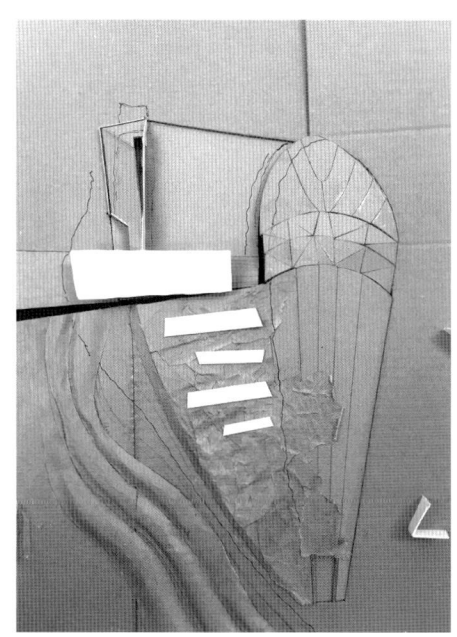

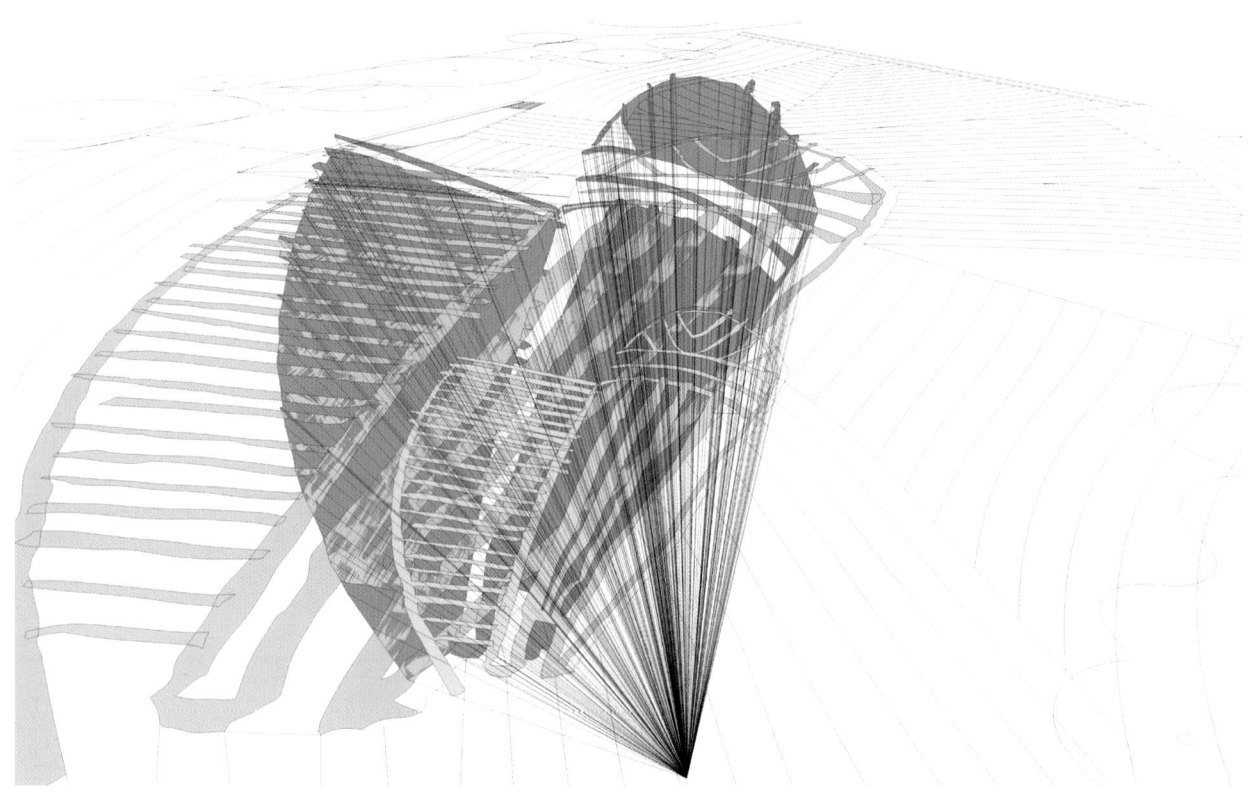

Anamorphic projection studies, Pavilion Landscape House

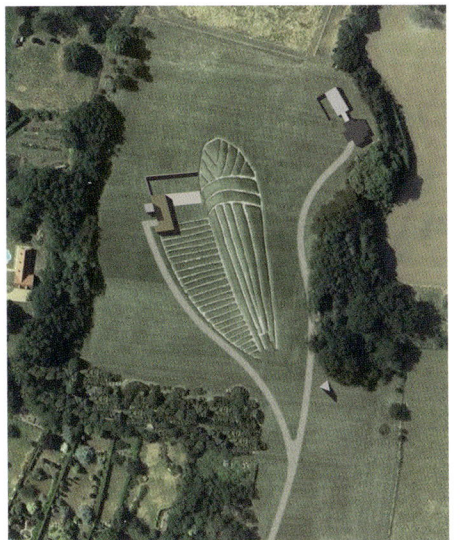

then meet, a tube of glue and scalpel in hand, to perform instant surgery on the model to take on board her latest thoughts, typically followed by a period during which she would reconsider and alter her drawings to take account of the ever-developing building design. We quite happily strayed into each other's territory—Whiteford proving a dab hand at clay modelling and we proving a useful ally in working out the geometry of the anamorphic projection.

Even though there is now a screen of trees between them, the main facade of the cricket pavilion addresses the manor mouse. We have restored this connection by building a ha-ha behind the pavilion, thus fictitiously redrawing the boundary of the manor house to include the pavilion within its curtilage. This boundary definition also serves to demarcate the parcel of land belonging to the pavilion, which will be in separate occupation, from that of the new house.

We have created a gentle hill in the middle of the site around which the site entrance drive bifurcates, giving a natural division of the site. To the right, the drive will trace the edge of the trees up to the old cricket pavilion and to the left the drive will hug the curved and rising edge of the artificial hill, leading to an opening in its side which is the entrance to the new house. The landscape hill and house sit comfortably towards the centre of the site, leaving a suitable margin to the surrounding boundary of tall trees and neighbouring houses.

The creation of the hill will be entirely from spoil generated by the reworking of the site. This will come from the ha-ha, from the basement excavation for the cricket pavilion extension and from the excavation for the new house. The landscape hill and surrounding territory will have a folded surface recalling local ridge and furrow fields, and will be grassed, with the lines from Whiteford's drawings picked out in white bonded gravel. The south-facing courtyard of the new house will provide adequate space for the paraphernalia of domesticity—barbecues, garden seating etc.

The original thatched cricket pavilion will be extended with a single-storey building, connected by a narrow link tucking in under the existing thatch eaves to the east side of the existing building. This will restore the best views of the pavilion, with the Burton manor house in the background, and allow the perimeter of the pavilion to be decluttered. Bedrooms will be in a basement below the new extension looking onto a sunken courtyard. The glassy ground floor will be simply an open-plan kitchen-dining space. A tall perforated field-stone wall to the south will screen the building from the manor house.

The new house is drawn from two traditions—one rural and one urban. It can be seen as taking up the themes of the English manor or fortified house. The use of earthworks has echoes of defensive ramparts and the inward-looking courtyard plan, accessed through a restricted gateway, is reminiscent of this type.

Top: Whiteford's site visualisation, Pavilion Landscape House
Middle: Lavender fields suggest ridge and furrow, Pavilion Landscape House **Bottom:** Mantling hawk

At the same time, however, the inspiration for the house is also quite urban, derived from a renaissance fortified townhouse or palazzo. The entrance is through a porte cochère into a private courtyard around which the accommodation is arranged. The major living space is on the first floor, accessed from a staircase opening off the covered courtyard entrance. What Nolli would have shown as the surrounding urban poché is in this case the earth of the artificial hill. This strategy delivers a practical yet highly dramatic entrance which allows for transition from the shady north-east side of the hill through to a bright, open south-facing courtyard, formally planted as a parterre to be designed by Whiteford.

The roof of the house grows specifically out of Whiteford's drawing, taking up the fanning feather-like shapes of the drawing and re-presenting them as a floating white shape hovering above the white lines drawn into the mound. It is distorted, like the drawing itself, and extends as an extraordinary cantilevered canopy over the entrance courtyard, gathering the smaller building elements beneath it.

The shell of the roof wing will be of polished fibreglass. The overall depth of around 2 metres not only allows the extreme cantilever but also forms a sufficiently rigid structure from which the open living deck can be suspended, giving a clear span over the pool below.

To the rear of the house the earth will be held back by a white concrete retaining wall, conceived as a vertical extrusion of the last of Whiteford's drawn lines down into the water of the pool. The natural thickening and thinning of her hand-drawn lines is exaggerated when they are projected anamorphically, so the vertical surface of the retaining wall will be as uneven as the drawn line from which it is generated.

The living space will be captured between the suspended deck and the light-reflecting roof structure. Sliding external screens will protect it from south-western sun. It will have long views, predominantly to the south, those to the west being limited by the hill. Both the living spaces and the pool will open onto the slightly sunken parterre courtyard.

Hidden within the band of trees to the east of the site will be a viewing tower from which the entire site—the land drawing, the two houses and the site entrance gate—will make sense as a single composition. There will be public access to the tower to view the project for a number of days each year.

Top: Compton Wynyates, Warwickshire **Bottom:** Filippo Juvarra, Palazzo Martini di Cigala porte cochère, Turin

Sigurd Lewerentz Woodland Cemetery complex, Stockholm

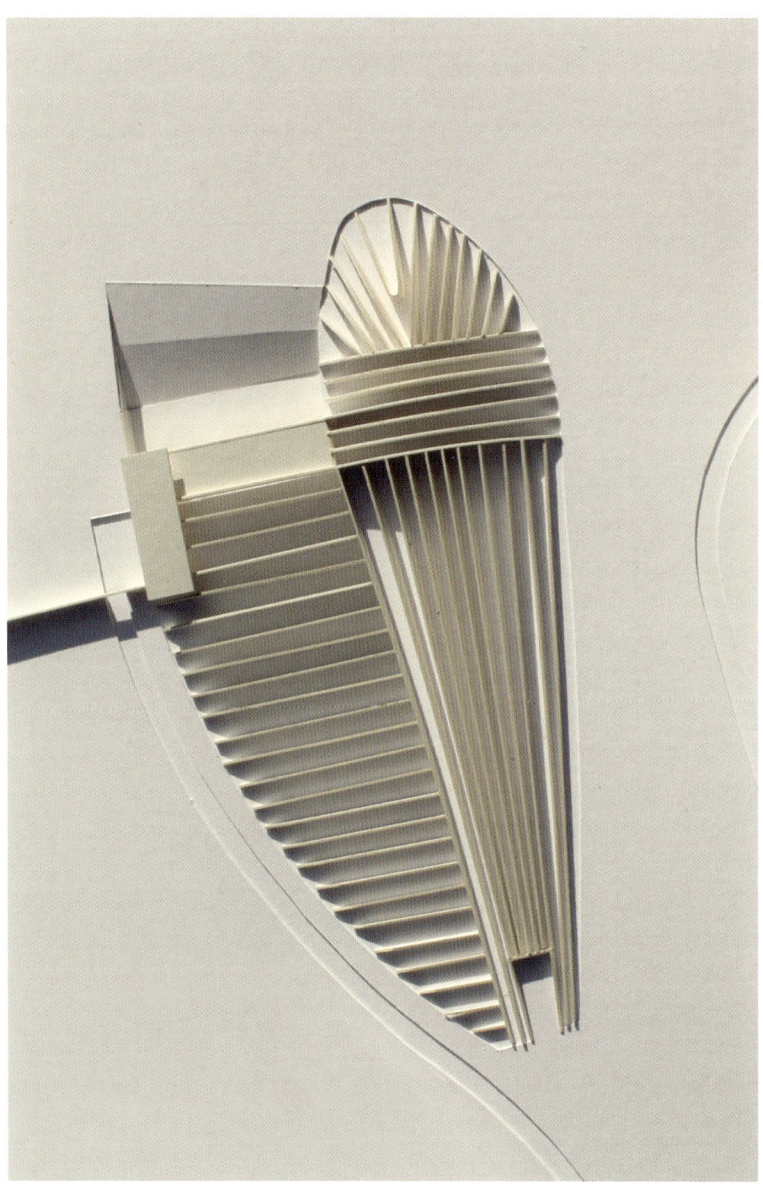

Above: White card rib model, Pavilion Landscape House
Opposite: Site model detail with Whiteford's chalk drawing, Pavilion Landscape House

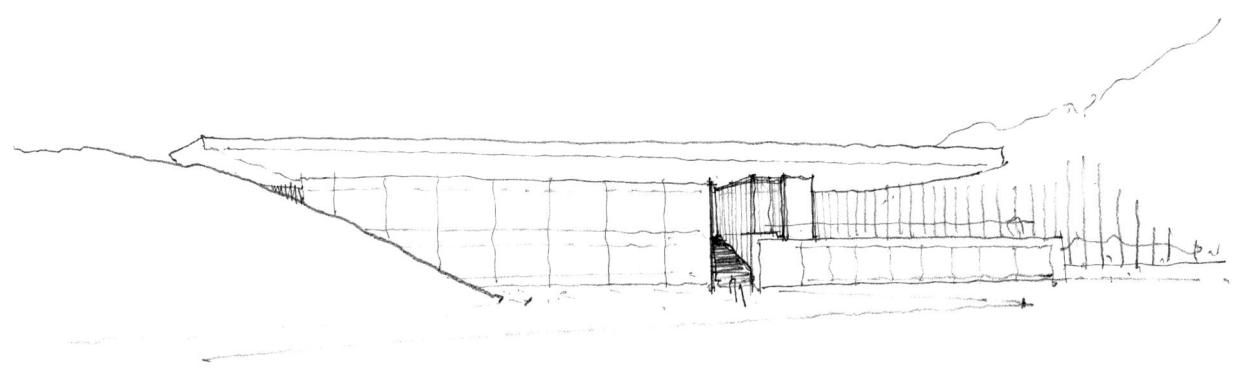

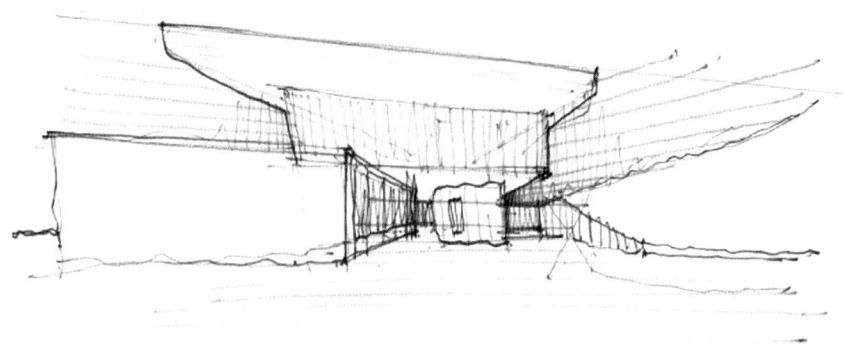

Top: View from courtyard, Pavilion Landscape House **Bottom:** View of porte cochère, Pavilion Landscape House

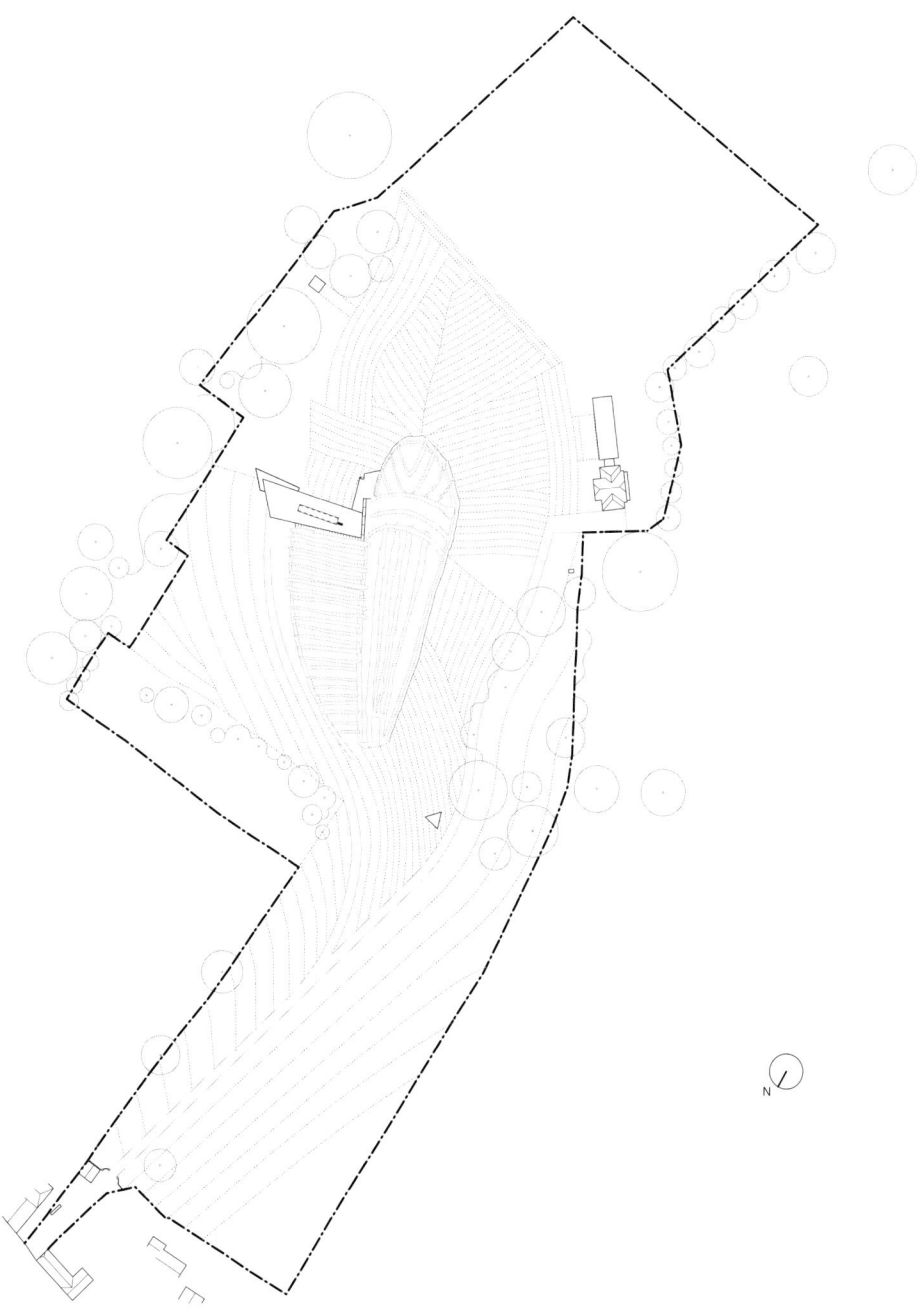

Site plan, Pavilion Landscape House

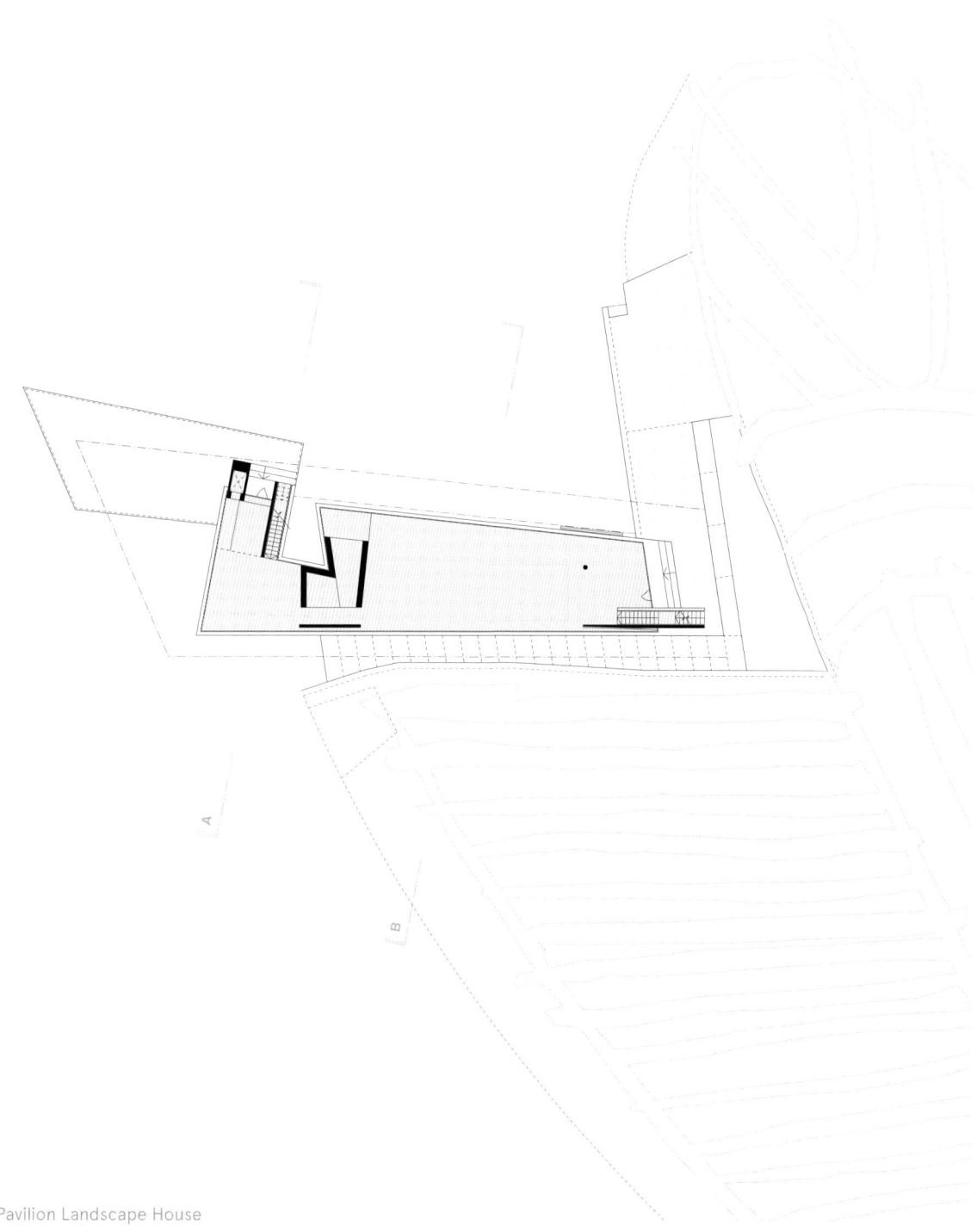

Site plan, Pavilion Landscape House

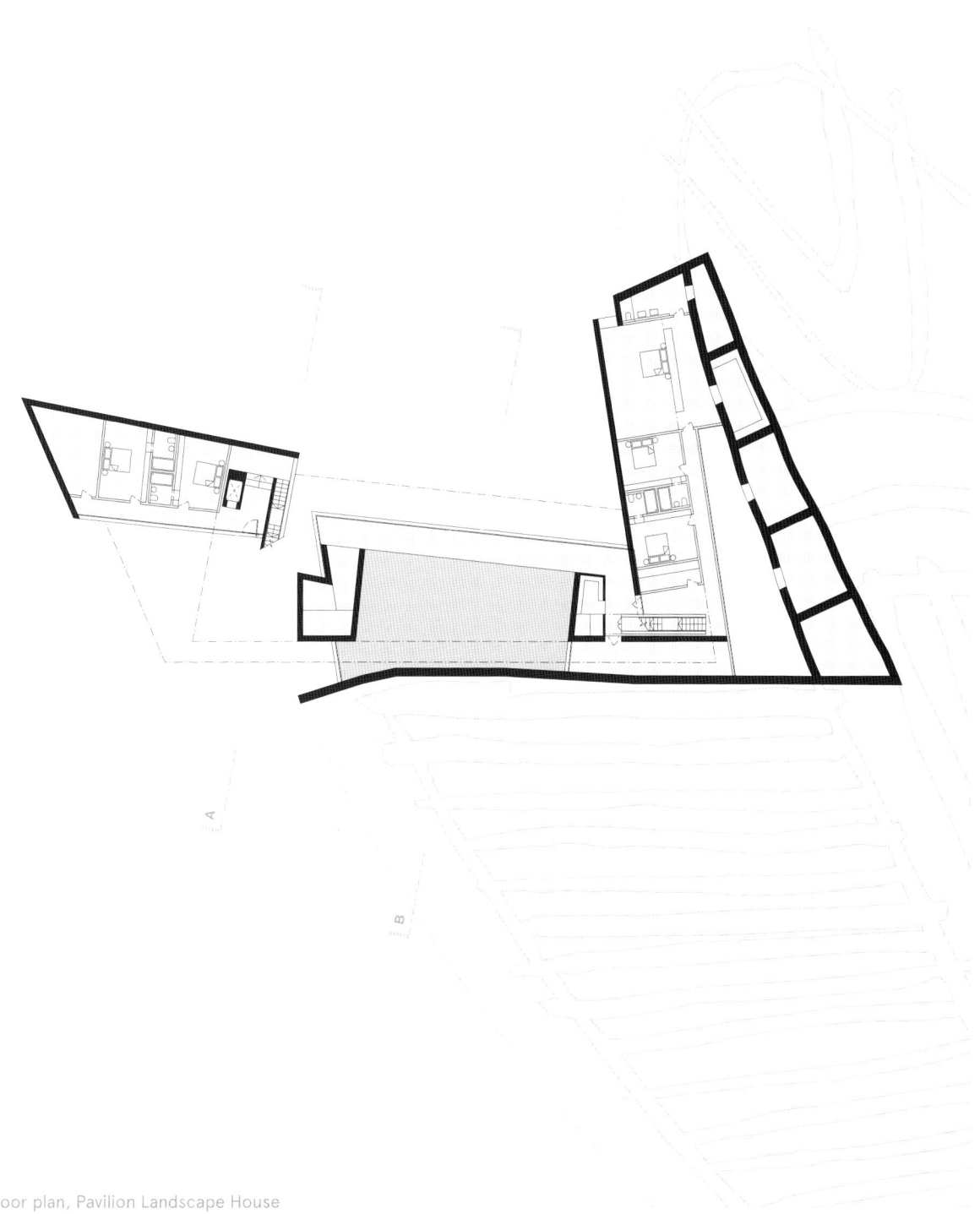

Upper floor plan, Pavilion Landscape House

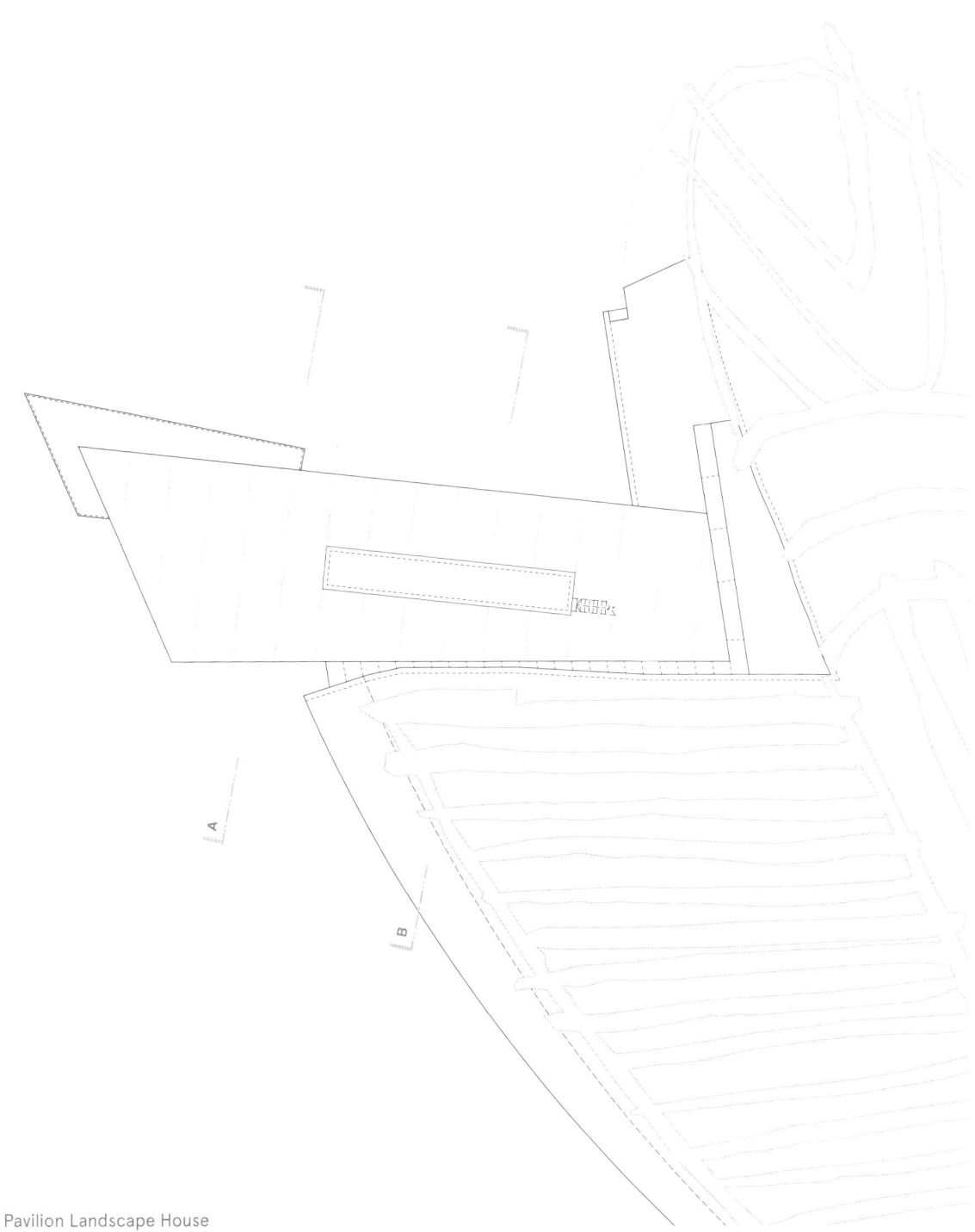

Roof plan, Pavilion Landscape House

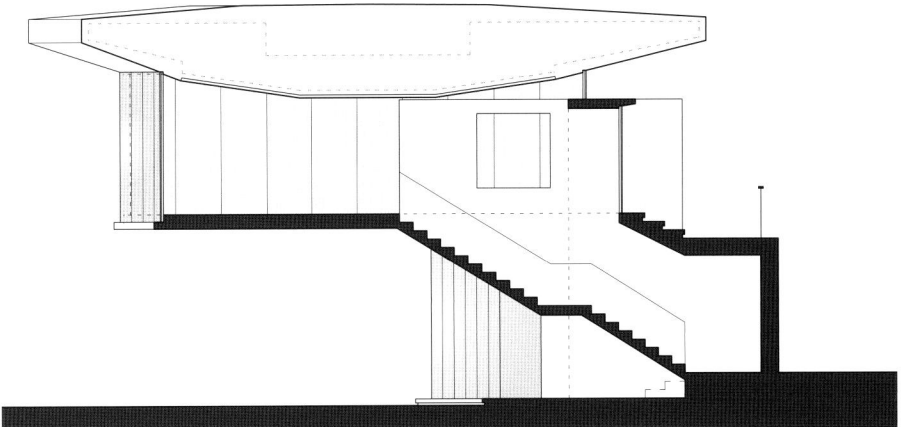

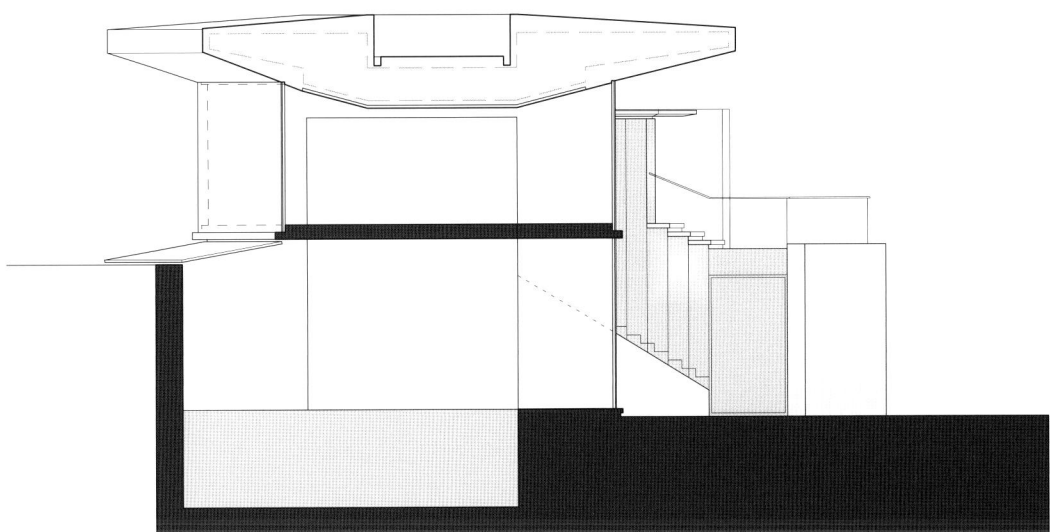

Cross sections through house, Pavilion Landscape House

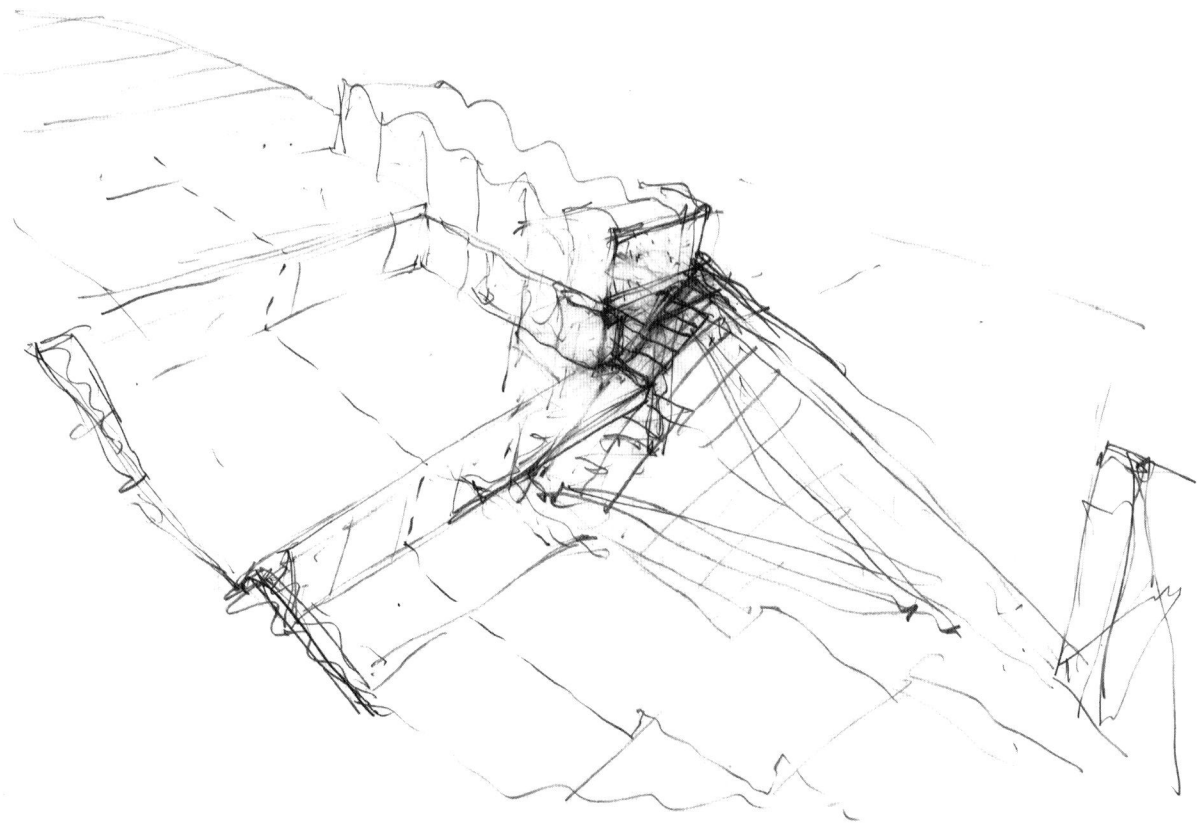

Concept sketch, Pavilion Landscape House

Site photo with sketch showing mound, Pavilion Landscape House

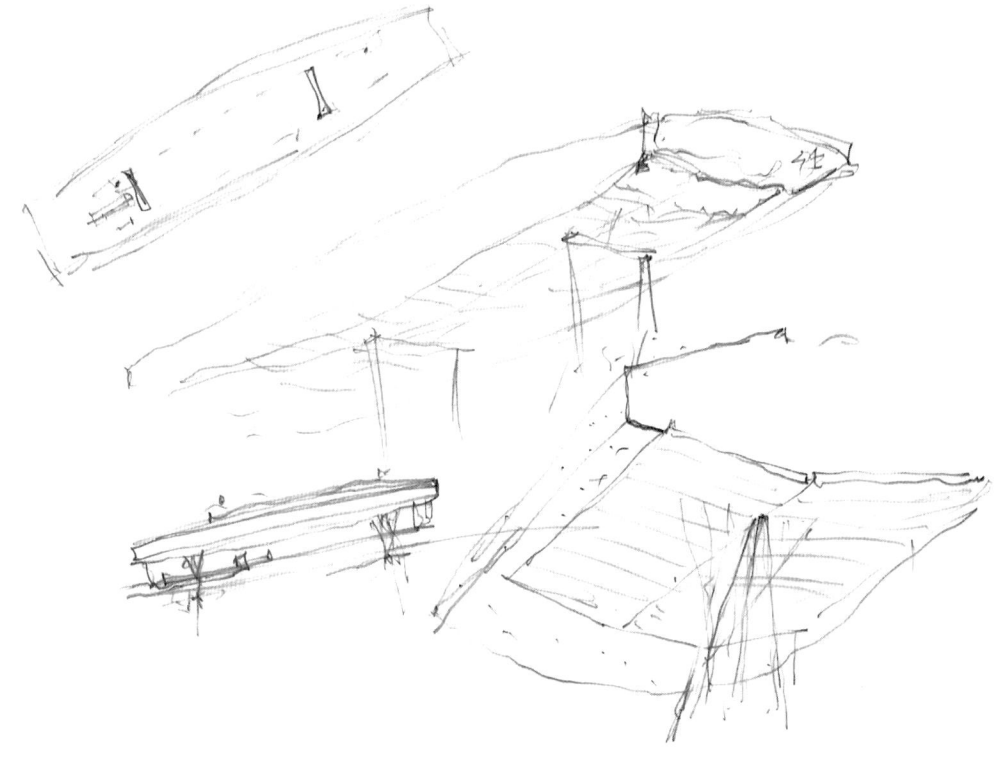

Roof wing sketch, Pavilion Landscape House

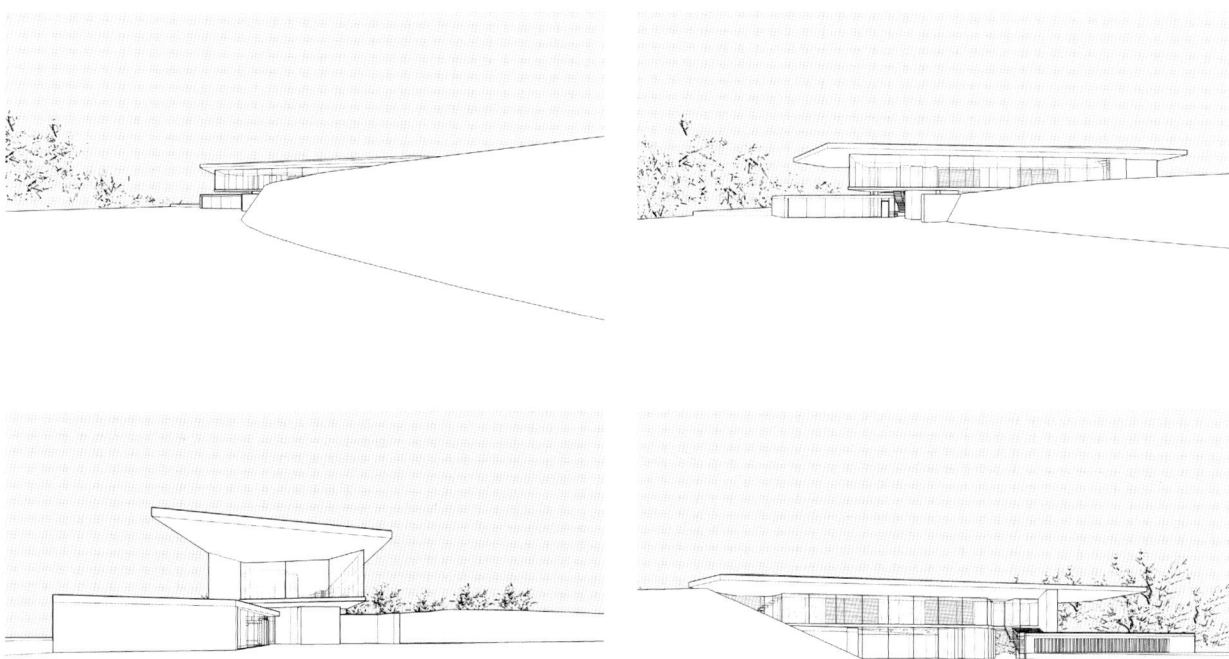

Views approaching the house, Pavilion Landscape House

Gentlemen and Players

Pierre d'Avoine

Joseph Rykwert in his essay, "Meaning in Building", has written that there is an acute need for architects to "acknowledge the emotional power of their work" and criticised their "preoccupation with rational criteria".[1]

Hugh Cullum, who studied at Cambridge with Dalibor Vesely and Peter Carl and subsequently worked with Colin St John Wilson on the British Library, would have known Rykwert, and has himself written that,

> I am quite happy to describe the way I work as more like feeling my way in the dark. The path is there and the objects to negotiate are real but they do not reveal themselves except by my reaching out tentatively until something tangible is discovered. Bit by bit the picture is built up, brought more sharply into focus and reviewed until the whole building is described.

Emotive power need not necessarily be about strength and force but even its opposite. In terms of Hugh's approach I imagine it to be about "sometimes rolling with the punches", about subtlety, responsiveness and fine tuning, which leads to a building whose outcome is uncertain even until a late stage. This uncertainty is both a sign of modesty and deep understanding. It is also, I feel, about the pleasure in risk-taking; the adrenaline rush of anticipation that occurs when design is understood as more than a preoccupation with rational criteria.

For the project at Hemingford Abbots, the task has been to evolve an approach to the wider landscape setting—it is never just a building—and the need to create a convincing narrative that has meaning for the multifarious protagonists in the project, some more important than others, some who may be just passing by, but for an instant may be rewarded with a flash of illumination no less intense because of its brevity. Hugh, in his approach to his work and the project for Hemingford Abbots, has declared an openness which could offer just such momentary pleasures as well as aiming for much deeper-rooted rewards, provided by a long-term relationship with the building and its setting.

In writing this essay, I am aware that Cullum and his collaborators are, after 16 months since inception, at the design stage when the proposal is still in a state of flux and that changes can and no doubt will occur as the design evolves. The commission has come about as a result of his long involvement with the adjacent site, a Decimus Burton manor house, where the practice designed a pool house and orangery, and recreated the walled garden in the grounds. The Hall was built for Rev J Linton by Decimus Burton in 1842–1843. It is a yellow-brick country house with hipped slate roof with modillion eaves cornice and central pediment to the west. It is currently Grade II* listed. The Burton manor house is fairly typical of a time before the Second World War when country houses could be built without the strictures of the planning system which came into place with The Town and Country Planning Act of 1947. The Act established that planning permission was required for land development and that ownership no longer conferred the right to develop land. At the manor house, Burton who was born in Loughton, Essex was free to draw on his repertoire which included Greek Revival, Georgian and Regency and produced a restrained Neoclassical house, set within a modest estate with no pretensions or scope to reconceive the wider landscape setting in the fashionable picturesque. However, its setting on the edge of the village of Hemingford Abbots, on the banks of the Great Ouse and part of the wider arable landscape, has its own 'found' picturesque quality which is still in evidence today. The estate included a cottage orné gatehouse, white-rendered and thatched, and subsequently a cricket pavilion built in 1897 in similar manner across the cricket pitch located opposite the garden front to the west.

The estate had been created by enclosing common land used for agriculture in the early 1800s. However owing to the creation of the manor house and its park by Burton in 1842, it was never extensively cultivated and there is still evidence of the ridge and furrow system used in open-field farming that took place throughout the Midland Plain prior to enclosure. The cricket pavilion, which is also listed, now forms a separate property and has been converted and extended into a residence. This building and its site is the subject of Cullum's project, following the invitation by the owners to work with them on their project, having been surprised by the success Cullum had with planners in the project he completed for clients at the manor house. The initial brief was to alter and extend the cricket pavilion, which had previously been subject to detrimental alteration and extension over the years. "The motive was not so much the need for more space as the need for a more practicable and workable plan." Several exploratory schemes to demolish the existing extensions and replace them with a single new one were abandoned owing to the way the proposed new extension imposed on the existing pavilion. Further attempts to situate part of the programme below ground so that the original building was returned to its almost symmetrical form led to the proposal to design a completely new house elsewhere on the site at some distance from the pavilion using legislation under paragraph 55 of the National Planning Policy Framework.

In recent years there have been a succession of government publications providing guidance on the design of houses in open countryside. "The Government Planning Policy Guidance 7: The Countryside – Environmental Quality and Economic and Social Development", published in 1992, was cancelled in 2004 and replaced by "Planning Policy Statement 7: Sustainable Development in Rural Areas". This too has been replaced by paragraph 55 of "The National Planning Policy Framework", published in 2012. The wording of these may vary slightly, but the main message is one of considerable resistance to building a new house in the countryside, whereas before 1947 it was considered a natural right of ownership.

Paragraph 55 includes the following clause:

Local planning authorities should avoid new isolated homes in the countryside unless there are special circumstances such as the exceptional quality or innovative nature of the design of the dwelling. Such a design should: be truly outstanding or innovative, helping to raise standards of design more generally in rural areas; reflect the highest standards in architecture; significantly enhance its immediate setting and be sensitive to defining characteristics of the local area.

The scope for interpreting paragraph 55 lies with local authority planning officers and national planning appeal inspectors. No more is the design of a country house a private conversation between architect and client. The process now involves intricate advocacy and lengthy negotiation. It involves the client in considerable expense and uncertainty. What generally ensues is a concerted local opposition and antipathy, and an unspoken prejudice against the sense of privilege and entitlement implied in the process, which is also understood as evidence of potential exclusion and participation in land that was previously common. For the cultural historian and literary critic, Raymond Williams, "the very idea of landscape implies separation and observation", meaning that landscape sets us at a distance viewing the world as scenery rather than as an immersive and tactile experience.[2] There is always tension between observation and inhabitation, although they are not mutually exclusive and both are inherent in the design process.

The site of the listed cricket pavilion lies just outside the village boundary of Hemingford Abbots. It is flat, not extensive and bounded to the north by rows of specimen trees, which are planted evidence of its recent use as a garden centre nursery until quite recently. The cricket pavilion site was never part of the Manor Hall estate but had previously been farmland.

For Cullum, unlike Decimus Burton who produced a relatively modest building fitting for its clergyman client in its setting, Paragraph 55 stipulates that "any new house should be truly outstanding, innovative... and reflect the highest standards in architecture... and simultaneously be sensitive to the defining characteristics of the local area." While these requirements are not necessarily contradictory or even unusual, indeed they would be desirable for any thoughtful, talented architect, it does set up another kind of tension when the design is subject to a different kind of expectation and intense scrutiny by expert officialdom and a wider public that could undermine a more subtle design approach.

It was this demanding context that led to Cullum's invitation to the artist Kate Whiteford, with whom he had previously collaborated on the British High Commission in Kenya in 1997, to work on a proposal which included the wider landscape of the site. Whiteford's practice as an artist includes a kind of land art that may be understood as a response to the ancient southern English landscape where the grass upland is cut to reveal the chalk and create symbolic shapes effective when seen from some distance, arguably the most notable example being the Uffington White Horse in Oxfordshire. Whiteford's work in this manner includes a spiral and giant fish artwork for Calton Hill in Edinburgh and for sites at Harewood House (after Chippendale) and Compton Verney (Airfield). Cullum has commented that, "Kate's projects do not work with the edges of a site."

John Wylie has written that,

> As an artistic genre and as a culturally conditioned habit of visual perception, one arguably unique to European and Western societies, landscape is a particular way of seeing and representing the world from an elevated, detached and even "objective" vantage point. It can be thought of as akin to other visual technologies (microscopes, telescopes, sextants) and modes of representation (cartography, architectural drawing) in which the world is conceptualized as an external, separate reality to be rationally perceived and accurately represented. Landscape thus belongs to science, rationality and modernity; it is the accomplice and expression of an epistemological model whose central supposition posits a pre-given external reality which a detached subject observes and represents.[3]

The move to combine building and landscape has led to a proposal to construct a giant mound on the field to the west of the cricket pavilion and to building a new house on and within it. Spoil for the mound would be obtained from the site itself where other earthworks would be dug including a ditch (ha-ha) or swale adjacent to the cricket pavilion forming the southern boundary to the project. It is worth mentioning that most of us, while not oblivious to it, tacitly accept that gigantic infrastructural earth-moves are involved with making new transport routes, embankments, cuttings and tunnels. Mostly the potential of these feats go unremarked except in the work of artists like Edward Burtynsky whose photographs reveal the dramatic beauty of these man-made landscapes and the spoil that is part of them.

Cullum's and Whiteford's project operates at an intermediate scale, but is still huge in comparison with the crick-et pavilion, where the mound is a manipulated landscape overlaid with symbolic markings and host to a dwelling house which appears to be parasitically attached to and within it. Cullum and Whiteford engage in a dialogue that also includes other protagonists: client, structural engineer, environmental engineer and landscape architect. The approach is synthetic and artificial although, paradoxically, the outcome aims at naturalness and, unlike the giant land artworks of artists like Robert Smithson, invites and ultimately relies on occupation for its affirmation and validation.

Cullum's process has included making a series of beautiful, brown card models to test the form of the mound and the way that the house may be positioned. These models have a lightness and deft abstraction that relate well to the cricket pavilion and its mock-Tudor black-and-white elevation. Whiteford, in the mean time, made a series of drawings of the mound overlaid with elemental patterns based first on the wing of a hawk and subsequently a cricket pad. Both these elements share the motif of subdivision into narrower strips formed by individual feathers or by the separated segments of the pad which allow it to be manipulated and wrapped around the batsman's lower leg. The design has meant a combination of the two complementary design initiatives and modes of representation and has now further evolved in a design which expands the pattern across the rest of the site to invoke the local ridge and furrow field system. There is an ambition to relate the design to the wider landscape including the grounds of the manor house and beyond. There will be limits to the application of the pattern and how it adjusts to existing features that are not within the control of the design team.

The village has a linear road running approximately east-west through it. The edge of the village to the south is held by the current field pattern and creates a stepped boundary. The approach-road to the site emerges south along a field edge and the new mound is placed with its narrow end sloping down towards the approach-road. Whiteford proposed a viewing tower be placed here to provide an elevated view where the pattern of the artwork is revealed. The entrance splits into two just before this point; the road to the right leading to the cricket pavilion and the one to the left hugging the long flank of the mound to the entrance to the house. The softer form of the mound gives way to more angular building—nothing is rectangular but the walls adjust forming an indent in the mound to accommodate the car park and entrance porch. A gap in the entrance wall leads onto a narrow south-facing terrace and access to the swimming pool, gym and garden room. The entrance hall leads to the bedroom wing and also houses the main staircase and lift that rise up to the living-dining-kitchen wing, laid across the top of the mound. From here there are panoramic views of the countryside under a wrapped-steel framed roof which is deep enough to accommodate a narrow terrace set into its top so that the occupants are more than half hidden when viewed from across the surrounding landscape.

The relationship between the various built elements in the landscape is still in a process of exploration. The new house exposed on its mound in dialogue with the cricket pavilion, the viewing tower and two smaller buildings on the edges of the site. Cullum has mentioned how "Frank Lloyd Wright has designed the same building but at different scales". There are comparisons with Taliesin West in the invention of a major element of the landscape. At Taliesin West it is the desert concrete, where Wright has cast boulders as aggregate into the linear retaining walls, which defines the layout and silhouette of the ensemble. There are parallels with the Lemoine House in Bordeaux by Rem Koolhaas, but without the structural gymnastics wrought by Cecil Balmond. At Hemingford the aim is more grounded, with the new house bedded into the mound, and even the mound itself has to be bedded into the site. The join between it and the adjacent land has to be contemplated and decided upon. The ambiguity of the roof over the raised upper floor has to be worked through. The original building was to be thatched like the original roof of the cricket pavilion and the roof of the entrance lodge to the Burton manor house.

Whiteford is carrying out optical tests, including anamorphic projection studies to establish the exact location, height and other parameters of the viewing tower, bringing the geometry of the wider landscape into play with the local geometries of the immediate site, the mound and the house. There are parallels with the work of the French sculptor and landscape artist Pierre Vivant who has worked mainly in Britain since the 1980s. His work too is about perspective and perception and includes a critique of food production on an industrial scale and the effect of this on the landscape and agricultural buildings within it. Whiteford's art practice is perhaps more literary and at the Hemingford Cricket pavilion site it involves a greater manipulation of the land itself as well as the visible layer of vegetation which implies a more coercive intention that blurs the boundaries between art, architecture and landscape.

The contribution of the landscape architect is yet to come and will have a significant impact on the evolution of the proposal. The rows of specimen trees on the north-west edges of the site are an awkward undesigned element which impact greatly on the narrative that Cullum and Whiteford have been carefully evolving. Can they be worked into the overall design or is their bounding presence too assertive for a proposal that aims for a diminution at the edges? However, the edges are important in a land system where parcels of land are defined by the way their edges are read. This is especially so in the flat landscape in which the site is situated.

The mound itself needs to evolve its narrative of construction. The barrows and tumps that are found in the prehistoric landscape are mainly associated with burial and funerary ritual. In England the most enigmatic of these is Silbury Hill near Avebury in Wiltshire. It too, like the proposed Hemingford mound is covered with grass. Its perfect flat-topped conical form is at first glance ambiguous, as to whether it is manmade or natural. It has long been known that it was constructed but archaeological excavation has not revealed its secrets and its function remains unknown, except that it is part of the ensemble of elements at Avebury which extend across the wider landscape of Kennet Valley and are now overlaid with the marks of contemporary agriculture, transport and settlement. The potential for the Hemingford mound to include voids, spaces for other, more ambiguous purposes within it has yet to be explored. The Egyptian pyramid is an obvious example, constructed on a vast scale, of an architecture that consists mainly of mass, but with precisely cut interior shafts, passages and burial chambers. The extended funerary landscape at Giza near Cairo, too, has been engulfed by the city, and its containment diminishes its power and potency. At Hemingford the outward-looking fancy of the prospect mound in the sixteenth-century English garden is brought to mind; examples include those at Wadham College, Oxford, Rushton Hall, Northamptonshire and Robert Smythson's Woolaton Hall in Nottingham where pertinently the house is built atop and within the mound itself.

The Hemingford mound house is a brave and potentially magical proposal that also brings to mind the Casa Ugalde House in Caldetas, 1951, by Jose Antonio Coderch. Here the site is high up on a hilltop overlooking the sea. The plan is non-rectilinear and the design spatially complex.

> Codech... along with the architect Manuel Valls (his partner) and the quantity surveyor Jusus Sanz Luengo, had direct control over the construction work, with the desire to improve such details as the actual act of building or the inspiration of the location might throw. In that respect it is important to note... just how many details of the work would have to be resolved in situ. The Casa Ugalde, however, is a work that is not definable in Euclidian, rational terms, having more to do with direct perception, with visual effects that can only be perceived in the reality of the site and which can only be created further to the project design, in the direct shaping of the building's form, details and finishes on the actual spot.[4]

In the project for the Hemingford mound house the effort put into the design speculations and initiatives through collaboration, testing and negotiation will have to be further tested through the process of construction and its relationship to the wider setting to result in a work of architecture, art and landscape that fulfills the generous ambition and open-ended aspiration of the processes that are being enacted.

1   "Meaning in Building", published in *The Necessity of Artifice: Ideas in Architecture* by Rizzoli in 1982, was initially commissioned by Eugen Gomringer for an anniversary issue of the *Basler Nachrichten*, but was subsequently rejected for publication.
2   Williams, Ramond, *The Country and the City*, London: Chatto and Windus, 1985, p 126.
3   Wylie, John, Introduction, *Landscape*, London: Routledge, 2007, p 3.
4   Montaner, Jose Maria, *Coderch Casa Ugalde House*, Catalonia: Collegi d'Arquitectes de Catalunya, 1998, p 32.

Further Reading:
·   Pevsner, Nikolaus, *The Englishness of English Art*, London: Penguin Books, 1964.
·   Hippisley-Cox, Robert, *The Green Roads of England Land Art in USA*, Glastonbury, UK: The Lost Library, 2010.

Opposite: Whiteford setting out the mound on site, Pavilion Landscape House

Chronology

Heath Street
Jeweller, New Bond Street
Doughty Street
Cove House, Cork
Decimus Burton Manor House
Fitzroy Square
Lancaster Grove
British High Commission, Nairobi
Genoa Avenue
Amor Road

Heath Street

Cullum and Nightingale

This was another project for the painter Shaun Stanley and his wife Fanny, who had bought a dilapidated collection of laundry buildings, some dating from the eighteenth century, at the end of a long passageway off Heath Street. One of the buildings was restored and became his sitting room and a small circular building was reconstructed as a helical staircase. The rest was new. To get light into the back of what was, of necessity, a single-aspect building, we put an open light-well and glass-floored circulation spaces towards the back and let the front face the large garden, mediated by a large orangery which Shaun needed to over-winter his more delicate plants. Many of the original external walls, which had become internal were left plain brick and they, with the reclaimed elm floor which was lovingly caulked with oakum (a task which took many weeks by a team including Shaun himself) contrast with the clean, bright construction of the ceilings and new walls. A great deal of effort went into hand-wrought details, such as the curved sliding maple screen, the retractable staircase to the living room gallery or the plant-like galvanised steel stems from which the roof of the orangery sprouts like some huge glass *gunnera manicata*.

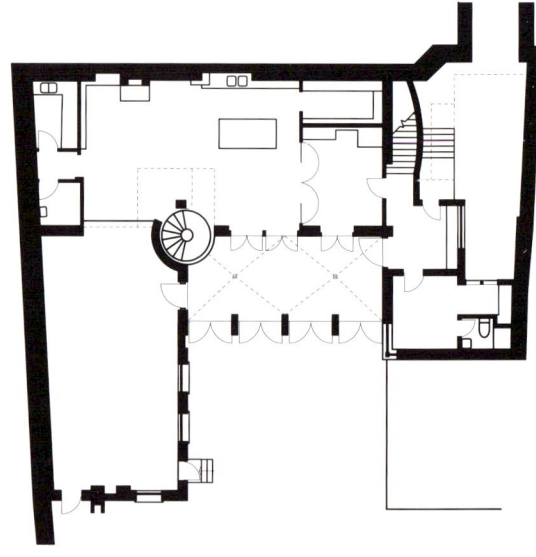

Top: Ground floor plan, Heath Street **Bottom:** Shaun Stanley, *House Construction*, Heath Street, gouache
Previous page: Conservatory, Heath Street **Opposite:** Stair in existing brick drum, Heath Street

Opposite top: Gallery becomes a stair, Heath Street **Opposite bottom:** Detail of gallery stair, Heath Street
Above: Helical stair from above, Heath Street

Opposite: House from garden, Heath Street **Above:** Toplight into back corridor, Heath Street

Jeweller, New Bond Street

This project replaced the former shop on the site, which we also created for the same client in 1996. It was a complicated development over three years, phased so the shop was able to continue trading throughout. Two adjoining shops retained facades, front offices and a double-height timber-panelled salon, for which a new, carved Portland stone shopfront was built. The use of beautiful materials and the quality of the detailing give it a presence that complements the expensive jewellery.

Top: Lacquer, Portoro and Calicatta marbles, Jeweller, New Bond Street **Bottom left:** Carved Portland facade, Jeweller, New Bond Street **Bottom right:** Bronze entrance detail, Jeweller, New Bond Street
Opposite: Interior in Elm panelling with lacquer and bronze detail, Jeweller, New Bond Street

Left: Bronze panelled stair hall, Jeweller, Tokyo **Right:** Exterior bronze screen, Jeweller, Tokyo

Rainy night exterior, Jeweller, Tokyo

Doughty Street

We converted this Grade II listed Georgian building from three flats into a single- family house. A large part of the work was the repair of the structure and the restoration of some of the fine period interiors. Where we have installed new bathrooms and dressing rooms, we have handled the modern elements as pieces of furniture, sitting within the period rooms that retain their original cornices, shutters and skirtings.

We have added a new garden room and kitchen, which opens onto a planted courtyard at the rear of the building. The contemporary style and lightness of the new spaces mark them as quite distinct from the rather formal rooms of the original house.

Above: Rear elevation, Doughty Street **Opposite:** Breakfast room, Doughty Street

Cove House, Cork

Shaun and Fanny Stanley, for whom we built a house and a studio in London, asked us to convert and extend three cottages belonging to keepers of a lifeboat station whose boathouse and launch ramp still form part of the property. It is a wonderful site in a bay off the sea surrounded by heather cliffs and headlands. The modest buildings will remain just that, letting the lush garden and landscape be the predominant voice.

The ground-floor front rooms of the cottages are made into a suite of living and dining rooms that give onto a terrace over the sea and we propose a further set of service rooms, kitchen, larder, laundry, etc, behind them, doubling the footprint of the house. On the first floor the strategy is repeated with the front bedrooms served by a new connecting corridor and bathrooms behind. Shaun is a great gardener and has made a beautifully planted south-facing retaining wall (a true vertical garden) at the rear of the house along the length of the site. With the boathouse to the east, this makes an entrance courtyard framed by a large pool, raised planting and tamarisks.

Above: View to sea, Cove House, Cork **Opposite top:** Overview of complete development, Cove House, Cork
Opposite bottom: Proposed view from pier, Cove House, Cork

Bracken inlet, Cove House, Cork

Existing house and outbuildings, Cove House, Cork

Shaun Stanley, *Hillside from the House*, watercolour sketch

Decimus Burton Manor House

With Jon Lowe of Heritage Collective, we have designed an orangery and pool house for this Grade II*-listed building by Decimus Burton. The pool house is conceived as a glass-house writ large, built on the perimeter of the restored walled garden but with a restrained yellow-brick pavilion addressing the landscape garden to the front of the house. The link back to the main house has been completed, as have replica roof lanterns over Burton's twin stair halls, and the restoration of the kitchen wing.

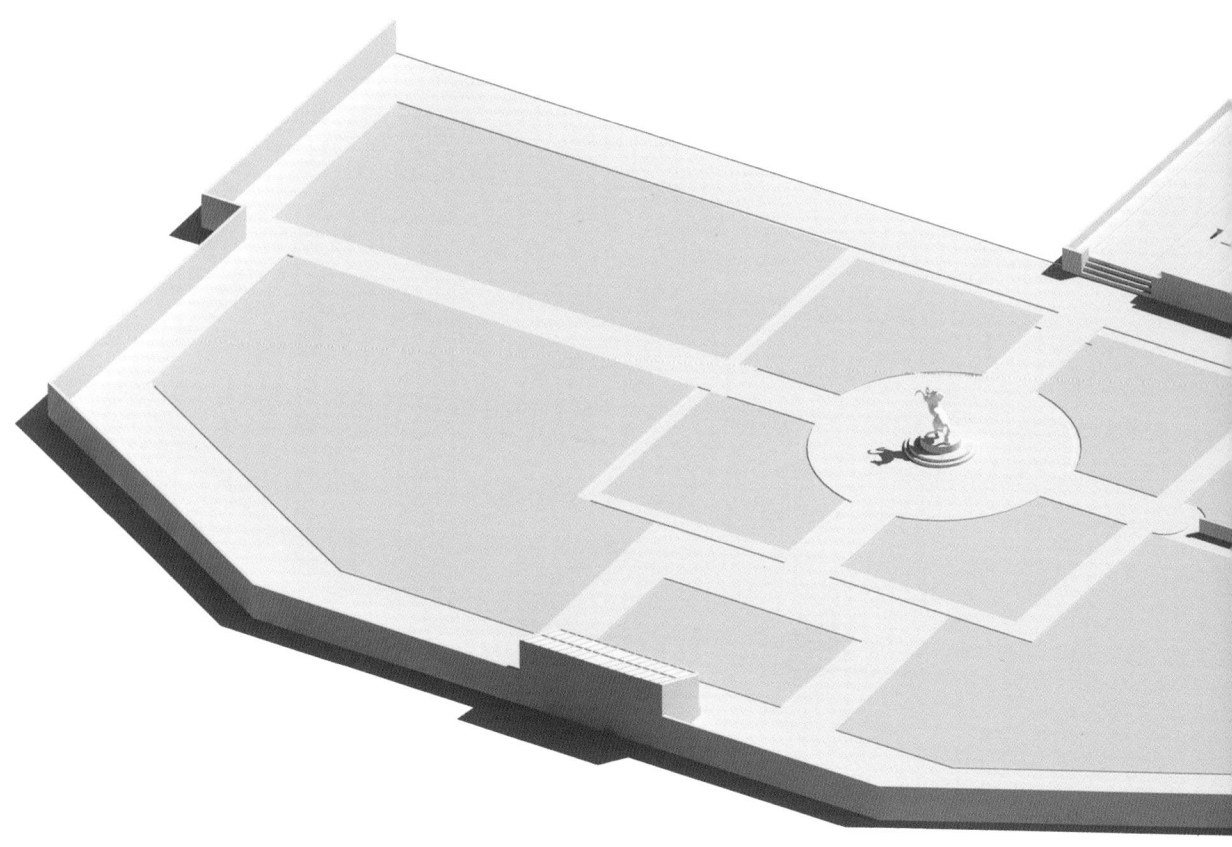

Above: Masterplan with pool and walled garden, Decimus Burton manor house
Opposite: Photomontage showing proposed garden pavilion, Decimus Burton manor house

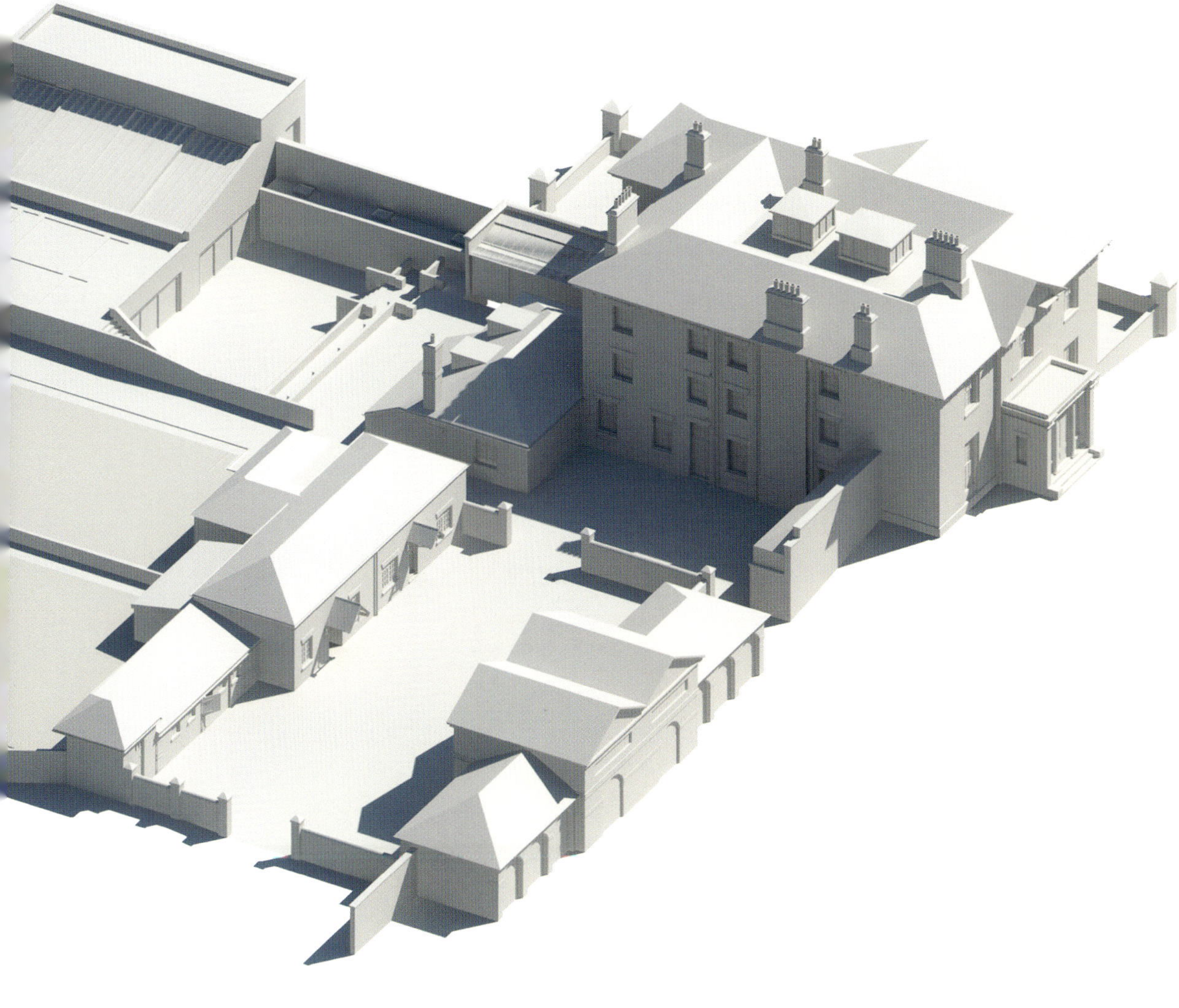

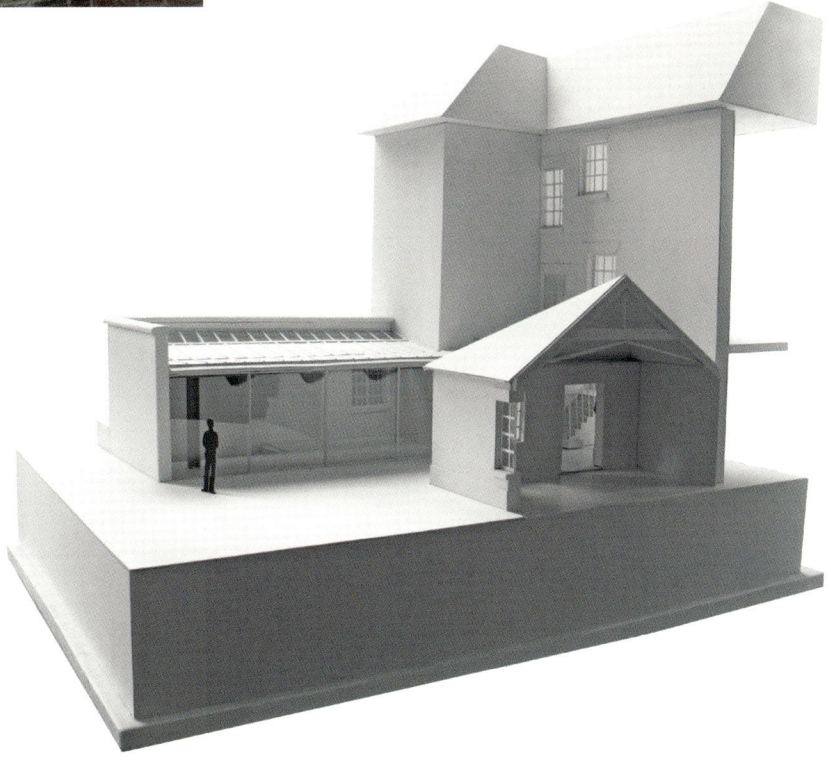

Opposite: Completed link building, Decimus Burton manor house
Top: Completed link building detail, Decimus Burton manor house **Bottom:** 1:50 card model, Decimus Burton manor house

Fitzroy Square

We are undertaking a careful restoration and refurbishment of this Grade I-listed town house by Robert Adam. This has involved unpicking the 'restoration' carried out when it became James Stirling's office in the 1980s and using the opportunities thus presented to introduce some unorthodoxies of our own, such as light-tunnels to get daylight deep within the building and the insertion of a panelled anteroom to connect the ground-floor kitchen at the rear with the more 'set piece' living room overlooking the square.

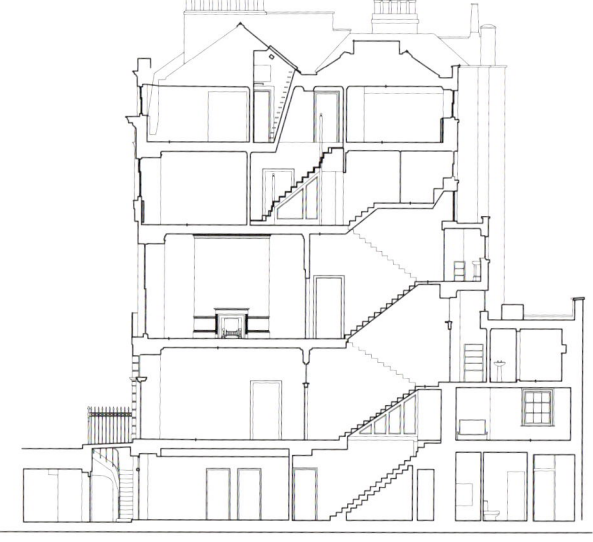

Left: Fitzroy Square **Right:** Section, Fitzroy Square
Opposite: Front elevation, Fitzroy Square

Lancaster Grove

The site was a car park at the end of a row of undistinguished 1980s terrace houses. Nonetheless it was within a designated Conservation Area and we had to demonstrate that the design fitted in, both in form and materials, with the prevalent local type of late Victorian bay-fronted houses. While this gave us a somewhat sober street faCade, the exposed flank of the building allowed a more inventive use of brick, following some lovely local examples of Edwardian rubbed red brickwork, and the possibility of a side- and top-lit staircase.

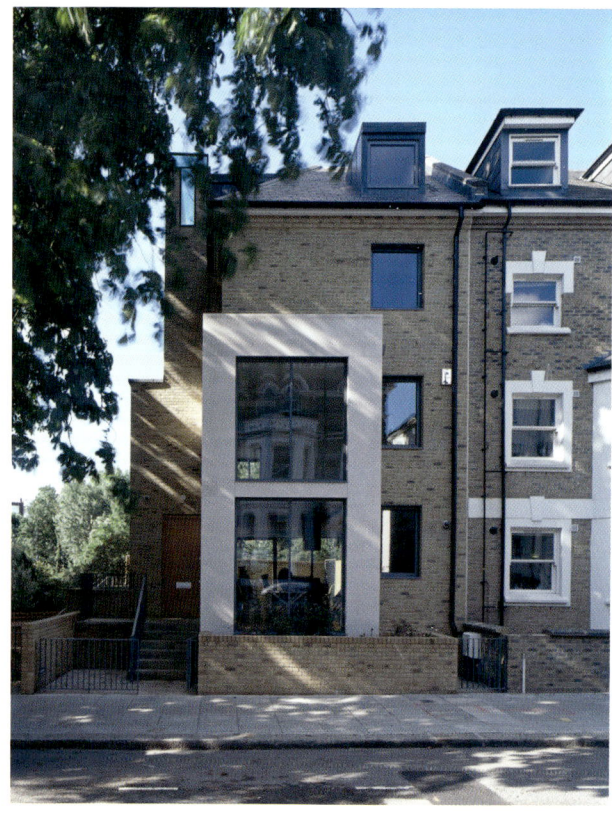

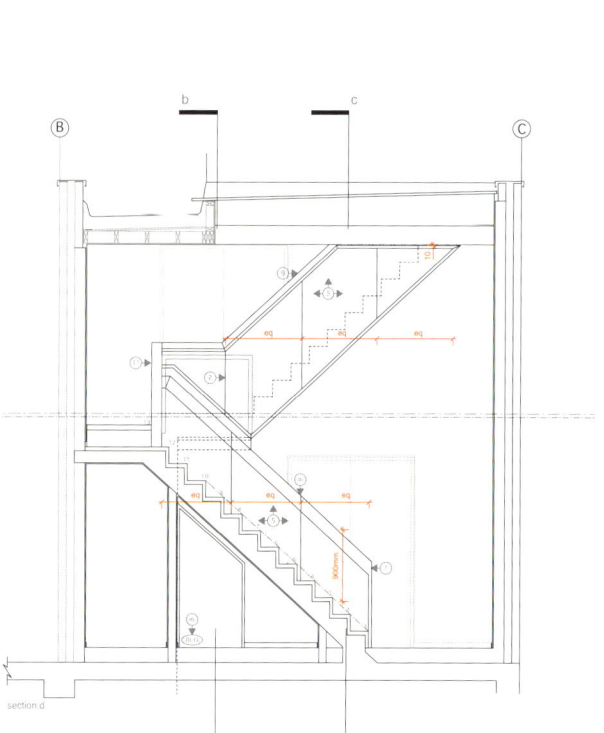

Left: Street facade, Lancaster Grove **Right:** Stair construction drawing, Lancaster Grove **Opposite:** Oak stair, Lancaster Grove

British High Commission, Nairobi

Cullum and Nightingale

Richard Nightingale and I ran a small practice with no experience of large buildings when we won the competition to design the new British High Commission, a major project which the Foreign Office, rather curiously, calculated to be worth around £8 million if it had been built in Milton Keynes. The parti was very simple and, we thought, symbolic of Britain's modern role in Kenya. The site is on a steep hill overlooking Nairobi and we proposed a building which was in two parts, corresponding to different diplomatic functions, connected by a high bridge to form an entrance portico. As one approaches the building the portico frames a wonderful view of Nairobi beyond, allowing the Kenyan capital to take centre stage while the framing building retreats to the wings. The construction is largely made up of load-bearing local volcanic stone, making it a massive and thermally stable building and allowing us to make great cliff-faces with the hand-cut but very finely jointed stone.

Top: Diplomatic wing from entrance courtyard, British High Commission Nairobi **Bottom:** Elevation overlooking Nairobi, British High Commission Nairobi **Opposite:** Entrance portico view to Nairobi, British High Commission Nairobi
Overleaf left: Axonometric of portico and entrance sequence, British High Commission Nairobi **Overleaf right:** Stairs to Diplomatic Wing, British High Commission Nairobi

Entrance Halls and Patio - British High Commission - Nairobi

Genoa Avenue

We aimed to bring the space and width of the garden into the interior of the house in this renovation and extension of a semi-detached villa in West Putney.

A line of tall brick piers define a permeable boundary between house and garden, creating a semi-enclosed courtyard placed between the new contemporary elements, the dining room and kitchen, and the original Edwardian house behind. Broad steps lead from the courtyard and terrace down to the lawn.

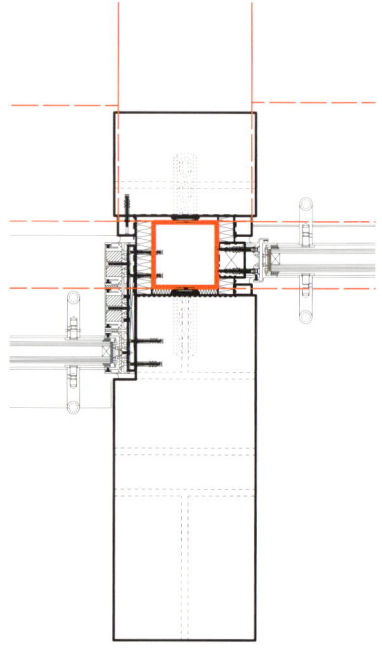

Top: Brick pier section detail, Genoa Avenue **Bottom:** View from garden, Genoa Avenue **Opposite:** Garden facade, Genoa Avenue

Amor Road

I have included this small project because it has worn well and continues to work much as it did when it was built 20 years ago. All credit to the client for insisting that she got what she wanted! It is typical of a number of refurbishments of London terrace houses that the practice has undertaken in the intervening years. The aim is to adapt these houses, with their cellular inward-looking room arrangements, for a way of life where the function of specific rooms has become more open, and the rear of the house, instead of being defined by the domestic activity of scullery, laundry and clothes-drying, increasingly looks towards a garden as a place of recreation and relaxation. As at Amor Road, this has often involved creating larger multi-use spaces and an attempt to give a level of natural light which approaches that of the garden to which it relates.

Left: Garden door, Amor Road **Right:** Garden, Amor Road **Opposite:** Kitchen, Amor Road

Acknowledgements & Credits

Thanks

In addition to patient and supportive friends and relatives I'd like to thank those who have taught me, those for whom I have built and those with whom I've worked. A great many of these have combined the latter three and in the process become the first.

Of particular importance have been:
Charles Cullum, architect and my father.
Peter Carl, PhD tutor and studio teacher.
Professor Sandy Wilson, teacher and my first employer.
Richard Nightingale, partner and co-designer for my first 20 years of practice.

I'd also like to thank my current co-directors and co-designers Stuart Everatt and Giles Woodcock and the team at HCA for their help producing the material for this book.

All of the featured projects have been the result of collaborative working and, having begun to assemble a list of those who have contributed, I've realised that the list is far too long and would inevitably be incomplete. Nonetheless, it goes without saying that I owe a huge debt to these past and present members of Hugh Cullum Architects.

Last but not least, I would like to thank Christiane Ten Hoopen for her support and friendship.

Biographies

Alan Powers writes and lectures widely on architecture, art and design. He teaches at New York University, London and at the London School of Architecture. His recent books include *100 Years of Architecture* (Lawrence King, 2016) and *Edward Ardizzone: Artist and Illustrator* (Lund Humphries, 2016).

Charles Rattray read architecture at the University of Edinburgh. He was in practice for over 20 years including a period in the studio of Sir Leslie Martin. For some years an editor of *Architectural Research Quarterly*, he is now a Fellow of the Geddes Research Institute at the University of Dundee.

Pierre d'Avoine runs an architectural office in London and practices internationally. He has taught at Bath with Patrick Hodgkinson, at the RCA, the AA, Kingston and currently teaches an MArch design studio at The Cass. He has been visiting professor at the Welsh School of Architecture (2002–2009) and guest professor at the Royal Academy of Fine Arts in Copenhagen (2009–2012). The work of the practice has been widely exhibited and published. Pierre co-authored *Housey Housey: A Pattern Book of Ideal Homes* with Clare Melhuish (Black Dog Publishing, 2005).

Well Mount Studio
Contractor: David Lightfoot
Structural Engineer: Sam Price

St Michael and All Angels
Contractor: David Lightfoot
Structural Engineer: Sam Price
Landscape Consultant: Jonnie Bell
Tile Maker: Phil Tomason
Client Representative: Peter Howe

Pavilion Landscape House
Artist and Co-designer: Kate Whiteford
Structural Engineer: Mike Shaw
Landscape Consultant: Jonnie Bell
Heritage Consultant: Jon Lowe
Planning Consultant: Holly Mitchell

Heath Street
with Richard Nightingale (Cullum and Nightingale)
Specialist Contractor: David Lightfoot
Structural Engineer: Sam Price

Jeweller, Bond Street
with David Collins Studio
Structural Engineer: Price and Myers
Quantity Surveyor: Peter Gittins
Services Engineer: Peter Deere
Stone Carver: Tim Crawley

Decimus Burton Manor House
Contractor: Tim Roberts
Structural Engineer: Price and Myers

Fitzroy Square
Contractor: Steve Clarke, SPC

British High Commission, Nairobi
with Richard Nightingale (Cullum and Nightingale)
Executive Architects: Hughes & Polkinghorne
Main contractor: Mulji Devrav and Brothers

Genoa Avenue
With Cheryl Knorr, interior designer

Amor Road
Contractor: Hill Heaton
Kitchen Joiner: David Lightfoot

Doughty Street
Contractor: Vitpol
Structural Engineers: Price and Myers

Photo Credits

Artifice books on architecture: pp 11, 81
Richard Nightingale: pp 12, 134–136
Peter Grant: pp 22, 36
Kate Whiteford: p 85
Lance McNulty: pp 44, 47, 48, 70, 107, 111–112, 132–133
Charlotte Wood: p 113
Terry Oborne: pp 114–115
Jon Spencer: pp 138–141

© 2016 Artifice books on architecture, the architects and the authors. All rights reserved.

Artifice books on architecture
10A Acton Street
London
WC1X 9NG

t. +44 (0)207 713 5097
f. +44 (0)207 713 8682
sales@artificebooksonline.com
www.artificebooksonline.com

All opinions expressed within this publication are those of the authors and not necessarily of the publisher.

British Library Cataloguing-in-Publication Data.
A CIP record for this book is available from the British Library.

ISBN 978 1 908967 82 4

Artifice books on architecture is an environmentally responsible company. *Topical Building: The Work of Hugh Cullum Architects* is printed on sustainably sourced paper.